Raising Mediators

How Smart Parents Use Mediation to Transform Sibling Conflict and Empower Their Children

Emily de Schweinitz Taylor

Mediator, Conflict Coach, and Mother of Five

Collaborative Book Works
EVERYDAY CONFLICT RESOLUTION

Collaborative Book Works

5387 S. Havana Court

Englewood, Colorado

www.collaborativebookworks.com

Edited by Leslie Watts

Cover Image and Design by Nada Orlic

Author Photo by McBoat Photography

Book Formatting by Damonza

PCIP Information

Names: Taylor, Emily de Schweinitz.

Title: Raising mediators : how smart parents use mediation to transform sibling conflict and empower their children / Emily de Schweinitz Taylor, mediator, conflict coach, and mother of five.

Description: First edition. | Englewood, Colorado : Collaborative Book Works, 2017. | Includes bibliographical references.

Identifiers: ISBN 978-0-9991717-0-7 | ISBN 978-0-9991717-1-4 (ebook)

Subjects: LCSH: Sibling rivalry. | Conflict management. | Communication in families. | Family mediation. | Interpersonal conflict. | Child rearing.

Classification: LCC BF723.S43 T39 2017 (print) | LCC BF723.S43 (ebook) | DDC 155.44/3--dc23

Published in the United States of America by Collaborative Book Works, an imprint of Em Taylor Communications, LLC. Emtaylorcommunications.com

First Edition

To my parents who taught me to care deeply about the world and to seek to understand all kinds of people. The time you spent with me as a child provides tremendous strength to me even today. May I pay your gifts forward to our rising generation of children.

CONTENTS

INTRODUCTION

It's summertime, and I've decided to take my brood of growing children to Costco because I thought it would be a quick, easy stop to pick up milk and other staples. As we move down the aisles of the vast warehouse thronged with people, my five children whirl around me. They are not just playing, but several are grabbing each other and actively blocking the aisle. What began as a simple task to get some milk has turned into a major sibling conflict with a large audience of disapproving bystanders who look my way, but avoid making eye contact with me.

Despite my desire to disappear from the mayhem, I am determined to continue until I have purchased the milk, which we need to keep things running smoothly at home. As my internal temperature increases, I recognize that I am both stressed and embarrassed to be in public while my children are fighting in a way that draws undue attention to our large family.

In public situations, when my children act against my

will and cause a scene, as they did in Costco, I have a visceral reaction of shame that rises in my belly and says, *Run! Hide! Take the kids and get out of here before you do something really embarrassing to try to control their behavior.*

Because I've read Brené Brown's groundbreaking work on shame, I realize that shame nearly prevented me from writing this book because parenting is messy business. Perhaps, like mine, your parenting journey has demanded the greatest sacrifices of your life and clearly exposed many fundamental weaknesses, as well as strengths, of your character.

Regardless of the risk I run in exposing my imperfect parenting to the world, I am convinced that the information I share in this book will help parents find better solutions to the conflicts they encounter in their daily lives with growing children.

*

Since my early days studying peer counseling in elementary school, I have been curious about and motivated to learn how to improve interpersonal relationships with others. Both formally and informally, I have pursued both academic and professional experiences that have helped me better understand the human experience in various cultures and time periods. I have studied anthropology, foreign languages, international policy and development, communications, and, recently, conflict resolution. My studies and professional experiences have taken me around the world to assist with political, non-profit, and corporate projects and relationships that include working with the Asian Pacific Economic Cooperation (APEC), the United Nations, and the World Bank.

However, despite my significant academic and professional credentials, my children test all my conflict resolution abilities, perhaps more than any person in the political or professional arenas I have experienced. Early on, as a new mother, I realized that I have incredible influence over the lives of truly remarkable little souls who rely on me to teach them about the world and how to successfully interact with others. Understanding that I am my children's primary role model, I have chosen to dedicate my greatest intellectual and emotional faculties toward understanding conflict resolution in the home: society's primary place of learning for children.

Focused on strengthening our families, I write principally as a parent concerned with alarming societal trends about how we manage conflict both publicly and privately. Like me, you may regularly witness a wide spectrum of ineffective conflict management. Out in society, we see how conflict goes awry, ranging from the tendency to avoid resolving everyday conflicts until they spiral out of control to the growing popularity of purposely creating contentions for entertainment's sake. Most worrisome, we cannot fail to notice a growing unwillingness to listen to anyone with an opposing viewpoint.

Writing this book has compelled me to face my imperfect parenting experiences and publicly share the knowledge and insights I've gained through diligent academic study of conflict in families. I am writing because these powerful ideas about parent-led mediation from my research and studies will benefit families so they can experience more peace and strengthen relationships with each other.

Regardless of age, situation, socioeconomic status, or education, most of us struggle to resolve the same kinds of sibling conflicts I encounter with my own children. Despite (and because of) my background as a conflict resolution specialist, I am convinced that every parent can model and teach effective conflict resolution to their children if they possessed the right tools. In short, conflict resolution skills should not be left only to the specialists, but need to be incorporated into the everyday teaching of parents with their children in the home.

As parents, I hope you will respond to the challenge of raising this much-needed generation of mediators among our children. Given the right tools, we can revolutionize the way our children face the future and give them hope so they can manage the conflicts that will inevitably come as they rise to lead their generation.

Raising Mediators explores how we can navigate the tension between our desire for quick peace and our children's desires for autonomy and independent decision-making. At its heart, this book is about how to balance our basic human needs and harness our capacity to move beyond win-lose mindsets about conflict, particularly in our homes. Through reading, reflecting upon, and applying the principles outlined in this book, we may discover our potential as problem-solving teachers and guides for our children. In short, we can learn to balance the autonomy needs of our children with our reconciliation needs as parents.

Nearly 80 percent of children in Western society grow up with a sibling, and that sibling relationship has a profound effect (good or bad) on each child's social development and achievement throughout a lifetime. In *Raising Mediators*, we acknowledge the experience of sibling rivalry for our children, but focus instead on how any kind of sibling conflict provides an opportunity for us, as parents, to intimately teach our children problem-solving, empathy, and perspective-taking skills. As a manual or workbook, *Raising Mediators* outlines how to position both parents and children toward sustainable, collaborative conflict management that outlines clear rules for engagement and strengthens our social development as individuals and as a collective family unit.

Like me, you may wonder if your children will respond to you as you move from the passive referee, invasive judge, or someone in between toward becoming a mediator or third-party communication assistant to your children. I understand and accept your skepticism. Your conflicts are seemingly intractable, your situations unique, but we all benefit from tools and ideas backed by new, but rigorous studies of hundreds of families with preschoolers to children in middle school. Let that little seed of hope—that we, as parents, do not have to coerce all peaceful solutions on our children—grow within you. Children can and often do learn to make wise choices on their own when we support them with guidance, modeling, and information about how they can talk with each other effectively.

Mediation is an extremely effective process that

allows people in a conflict to be guided towards their own solutions by a third party, the mediator. In mediation, the conflicts do not run you, but you channel the energy of the conflict through an effective collaborative communication process that involves listening, restating, and reframing individual concerns as joint problems to be solved. Essentially, mediation has the potential to convert conflict crisis with win-lose stakes into true opportunities to teach critical problem-solving skills and empathy. As parent mediators, we help create a communication process as a scaffold that allows children who are fighting to do the following:

- Establish rules and roles for each other in a fair process .
- Share perspectives and understand each other's emotions
- Reframe conflicts as joint problems
- Brainstorm solutions to shared conflicts
- Jointly select solutions that reflect the interests of both children
- Reality test the possible effectiveness of a chosen solution

You may be worried about your lack of specialized skills or limited time, but becoming a parent-mediator will not require thousands of dollars, years of study, a graduate degree, or even a deep philosophical understanding of mediation principles. As a step to becoming an effective parent-mediator, we must first learn about our own conflict patterns. We then set to work developing specific parenting habits and perspectives within a clear, fair communications framework. While mediation skills and principles may go against common parenting practices, mediation incorporates many familiar, effective communication tools that we already know from everyday life.

Despite our different personalities and childhood experiences, parents can each change their conflict resolution habits through conscious effort and learning. Even as adults, we are capable of changing our habits because we are not merely the product of our genes, previous life experiences, or even our basic temperaments. The way we behave when we face a conflict is often less about our personalities and more about what we saw adults do and how we were treated as kids. That said, our children benefit even more from learning more constructive communication skills from a very young age because of their great brain flexibility. Research shows that even children as young as three years old can mediate conflicts with their older, more socially-savvy siblings.

Certainly, we face many obstacles to becoming effective parent-mediators. Research suggests even parents have a hard time not taking sides or being neutral about our children's conflicts. Also, we often struggle to listen to our children when dealing with sibling conflict, fail to listen to each child impartially, and favor our own ideas over our children's less elegantly expressed opinions. Most importantly, we tend to want immediate solutions to resolve sibling conflict quickly.

Yet, true successful collaboration through mediation takes more time (and patience) as a parent than either telling kids to work it out themselves or trying to resolve it ourselves.

However, we can overcome these obstacles through effort, learning, and some trial and error on our part. Over time, becoming a parent-mediator requires that we learn to withhold initial judgment, facilitate rather than dominate a discussion between our opposing children, resist forcing solutions upon them, and allow kids to craft their own solutions within appropriate frameworks and family values.

Mediation doesn't work for every conflict situation, nor is it designed to resolve every kind of conflict. There are pros and cons to each of the five general conflict resolution approaches that we will explore in chapter 2. Even without using the full process, certain elements of mediation make sense to implement right away to improve basic communication among family members. The more we use mediation, the better we'll be able to judge its effectiveness.

As I have begun my own journey toward raising mediators and becoming a parent-mediator, I have asked myself the following fundamental questions about teaching my children conflict resolution. To prepare your mind to learn about parent-led mediation, how would you answer the following questions?

Workbook Questions:

- If I don't teach my child how to resolve conflicts successfully at home, where is he or she going to learn it?

- Right now, what are my children learning about conflict resolution (feelings, thoughts, and practices) from me and other adults they spend time with?
- What are my greatest concerns about conflict resolution in our home right now?
- What do I hope my children will learn in our home about conflict resolution?
- What current habits am I willing to change to learn how to mediate my children's conflicts?

The individual chapters within *Raising Mediators* can be read on their own when you want to focus on a particular topic, but I suggest that you first read through the whole book once and then revisit individual chapters as desired. Each chapter of *Raising Mediators* includes questions to help prepare you for the chapters that follow and practical home application of parent-led mediation processes and principles. These questions are phrased for an individual parent, but are just as appropriate to answer in conjunction with others.

Book Layout

As you read, you will hear my voice and many of my personal thoughts and experiences. To maintain the privacy of my family, I focused on my own parenting experiences, rather than my husband's. I do refer to many experiences with my children, (but have changed their names to avoid embarrassing them). But, this book is not about me. I have written this book as a practical guide for parents with helpful and actionable information that you can use in your daily lives as parent-mediators to teach your children effective problem-solving skills. I reference works by conflict resolution specialists in the resources section in the appendix so that you may expand upon the ideas I have presented and cater them to your individual needs. To help you apply the principles in each chapter, I've included exercises you and your family can use to practice conflict management skills.

To create a framework for the discussion about conflict management in the home, in chapter 1, I show you what conflict is and how it begins. With this understanding of what fuels your children's and your own hostile feelings and conflict behaviors, chapter 2 reveals the five general conflict management approaches. In this chapter, you'll find definitions, the pros and cons, and the ideal conditions for using each of the five general approaches to conflict. These include avoiding, accommodating, compromising, competing, and collaborating. In chapter 3, I provide real life examples of using the five different conflict approaches with conflict in my own life. From these three chapters focused on how we approach conflict, I move into sections focused on understanding and managing your children's conflicts with each other.

In chapters 4 and 5, I lay the groundwork for understanding where parent-led mediation fits in your overall conflict management approach with your children. First, I share child development research that helps clarify what your children are capable of given their socio-emotional and intellectual development. Next, I investigate the importance of the sibling relationship and the role that sibling conflict plays in your children's development.

In chapter 6 and 7, I help you analyze how you manage conflicts with your children. You'll see patterns of intervention (or nonintervention) and beliefs about your children's conflicts with each other. Throughout this section on parental practices and beliefs, you will have the opportunity to explore your own thoughts, feelings, and motivations about your children's conflicts. To outline key areas of parent preparation for managing your children's conflicts, I refer to the acronym TEACH ME, which is reused with different meaning in the parent-led mediation training section.

In chapters 8 and 9, I lay out the process of parent-led mediation using the TEACH ME acronym to explore the seven specific steps of parent-led mediation. Chapter 8 focuses on the mechanics, while chapter 9 shows you how to implement parent-led mediation in your children's more intense daily conflicts and how to use a simple conflict matrix to analyze your children's more intense, recurring conflicts. I also compare conflicts where parent-led mediation is beneficial with those that do not warrant collaborative problem solving with parents.

In chapter 10, I share the four fundamental family practices that support (and prevent the need for) effective parent-led mediation practices in the home. These four practices include: building parent communication skills, holding regular family meetings, establishing and upholding family rules, and practicing clear, compassionate communication. The practices strengthen families and may be adapted to other social contexts to enhance constructive communication.

Finally, in the conclusion and appendix sections, I summarize key research included throughout the book in chapter-based notes and provide recommendations for further reading. While not exhaustive, the resources section provides information to help you find more academic research on key topics, such as the sibling relationships, sibling conflict, parent intervention, and parent-led mediation.

While *Raising Mediators* is not the final word on parent-led mediation, I present parent-led mediation as a new way of looking at and responding to your children's conflicts with a collaborative mindset. Perhaps, the collaborative road less taken in resolving sibling conflict has just been hidden from view until now.

I hope that, in the years to come, parent-led mediation will make a great positive difference in how we, as parents and children, treat each other and experience our home lives together. Small, daily efforts to teach constructive communication at home can revitalize a society riddled with misunderstanding and violence. Whether we recognize it or not, we have the opportunity to raise the next generation with the necessary skills and attitudes to resolve pressing issues and needs both at home and abroad. Never underestimate the power of your influence as a guide and teacher to your children, who are your most important students in this life.

CHAPTER 1
AN OVERVIEW OF CONFLICT

In some ways, talking about conflict is like discussing waste management. No one really wants to talk about dirty water until we reframe the discussion as one about producing clean water. Likewise, we often feel more comfortable turning a discussion about conflict into one about peace-making or getting along. Whatever way you choose to spin the topic of conflict, it helps when you first frame conflict for yourself, looking at your thoughts and feelings before turning to managing your children's conflicts. Pay attention to how even a discussion of conflict makes you feel as you read the following passage.

My heart is racing, and I am trying to leave the building as soon as possible. I have just tangled with my supervisor about a sensitive staffing issue in front of our bosses, and I can still feel the emotional tension mounting inside me as I move to release myself from the awkward situation.

Following this painfully tense interaction with a woman whom I've disagreed with occasionally in the past, I'm trying to get out, to breathe, to think a little, to regain my equilibrium. But, my adversary is trailing me—she wants to talk things through now. She is calling my name and has nearly caught up with me as I enter the parking lot. I'm not ready to talk calmly with her. With all my training in conflict resolution and communications, I still do not want to have this conversation. I am not ready because my feelings are still bubbling up inside of me. I am all emotion. I can see my car, but she is right behind me, ready to open the "conversation."

Tired, hungry, and a bit humiliated by how she verbally shut me down in front of our bosses, I dread the coming confrontation. She is only steps behind me, and ready to talk. I am like a bomb ready to explode. My car is so close, but she digs in and opens the conversation before I can climb into my car and escape. I have tried to keep the emotion down, but once she starts asking me what happened inside the office, I start rattling off how angry I am. Without a lot of thought, I unload my feelings of discouragement, of upset, of misunderstanding, of frustration. I am like a volcano at first eruption. The barriers of social decorum crumble and the lava of contention unloads. The tension is tangible. She is not smiling any longer, but looks concerned and frustrated like me.

Naturally, she reacts to my words and frustration defensively because I lose my cool and start blaming her rather than expressing my true needs. I open my car door and try to cut off the conversation, but she persists in talking without a natural pause. At this point, nothing I say is helping to soothe hurt feelings. I apologize for the confrontation that embarrassed her in front of our supervisors, but she will not allow me to leave; she seems fully engaged in the conversation. When I am finally in my car with the door shut, but the driver's window rolled down, she asks for more time to talk. In a flash of wisdom, I ask if we can talk more later so I can eat, reflect, and ponder our fight.

Finally, she relents and agrees to talk more about it later, releasing me from this shameful interaction. As I drive home, I am in shock, holding back tears until I reach home. I quickly run up the stairs to my bedroom where I release my outrage with crying and expressions of humiliation that instantly surfaced within me during this encounter with my boss. I am angry at her, but also angry at myself for losing my cool. I wanted to escape before I exploded, but I couldn't get away in time.

When conflict arises, I don't usually explode, but this particular situation left me feeling out of control and then ashamed for not containing my emotions and not meeting my own needs effectively. Even in my forties, I am still learning how to manage conflict in my professional and personal lives, which reminds me that I will be fine-tuning my communication and conflict resolution skills my entire life. The thought that I am a work in progress is both discouraging and hopeful at the same time. While I am more familiar with my weaknesses as I grow older, I am also more confident that I can gradually improve, too, because I notice that I have changed in positive ways.

As you remember experiences of conflict and the feelings that accompany successful and unsuccessful attempts at resolution, you develop greater empathy for what your children experience in working out their differences with each other. To help your children understand how to manage conflict, in this introductory section of the book, I first examine how people think and feel about conflict themselves—beyond the emotional understanding that they are in conflict with something or someone. In the second chapter, I identify general conflict management approaches alongside certain patterns and beliefs that parents hold.

The Feelings of Conflict

Most likely you are very familiar with the negative feelings (i.e., tension, anger, fear, and shame) that may accompany conflicts. Your blood pressure rises, your chest tightens, your rational brain shuts down, and high emotion reigns. Not all conflicts evoke these strong responses, but you understand these visceral, emotional responses to conflicts that truly matter to you.

Despite your recognition of the emotions evoked during the middle of conflict, you may be less conscious of (1) the thought processes that create conflict and (2) your own unique patterns and beliefs about responding to conflict.

For example, in the conflict with my coworker, I knew for sure that I was angry, but only with time and reflection did I sort out what particular issues had fueled my strong emotional response and hostility toward my coworker. At heart, I felt slighted and unimportant when my opinion was not fairly considered in a decision-making process that directly affected my activities and staff. Ultimately, I had to become aware of how the conflict began to appropriately process my hostile feelings and strong emotional reaction to my coworker's behavior.

Significantly, your own conscious understanding of the origins of conflict and your general responses to conflict help prepare you for using conflict management tools, such as mediation, with your children. As the primary teachers of your children, you have a unique opportunity to directly assist them in understanding how to manage both their feelings and conflict behaviors. You take the first step in helping your children resolve conflict by becoming consciously aware of definitions, conflict thought processes, conflict origins, and some general cultural assumptions about conflict.

The Thought Processes Behind Conflict

The Central Tension: Balancing Individual Needs with Desires for Social Belonging

To understand what drives our conflicts, we first reflect on our natural wiring for both individuality and social connection. Regularly, we experience this tension between meeting our personal needs while also securing social connection with others. Every day, we naturally experience "differences" or friction that threatens the delicate balance between meeting individual needs and desires while maintaining social connection.

For example, in one moment, I want to read my book in silence (individuality), yet fifteen minutes from now, I may long to have a conversation (social connection) about what

I read to feel connected to my spouse, friend, or children. Similarly, our children may like to play with their Legos in the presence of siblings without sharing them as evidence of both getting what they want individually while enjoying the company of others (social belonging).

Some periods in our lives allow for greater attention to meeting individual needs over making social connections. For example, when I was single, I could travel, shop, and sleep in whenever I wanted to (as long as I arrived at work on time). Now that I am a mother, I constantly have to squeeze in my individual needs to meet the demands of a large family. With more frequent and close social interaction at home, I know that I enter more regular, ongoing conflict situations now than before having children.

The natural tension between desiring both individuality and social belonging on occasion means I want both needs satisfied at the same time. Simultaneous occurring desires usually require that I settle the internal conflict by choosing what matters most at a given time. For example, sometimes I can't read my book quietly while sitting in the living room with balls flying over my head and the chaos of boys exchanging Pokémon cards on the floor beneath me.

In short, despite the various roles we play and the different relationships we enjoy, all of us, both parents and children, constantly balance this internal tension of individual desire versus social connection. Considering this tension, we should not be surprised that in almost every human relationship (even with ourselves), we experience conflict.

Researchers have described this tension between individuality and social belonging in terms of *assertiveness* (seeking to satisfy your own goals) and *cooperativeness* (seeking to satisfy others' goals). We are wise to recognize these competing desires in ourselves and in every other person we meet. This central tension underlies all discussion of conflict and our various approaches to conflict management. In chapter 2, I explain how the five basic approaches to conflict differ in satisfying these competing desires to achieve both assertive and cooperative goals.

Defining Conflict

Conflict may simply be defined as "differences that matter" to one or more parties. Given this broad definition, people may become involved in a conflict unknowingly because another person assumes a difference. Have you ever learned that someone had a problem with something you said or did, but you were completely unaware of the offense? Have you ever forgotten to return something you borrowed only to find out that the person who lent it to you had been silently seething for months?

More specific definitions of conflict focus on identifying both *what we do* and *the negative feelings we experience and express*. The mere appearance of conflict may deceive us because we misunderstand other people's goals. Simply put, conflict theorists, Kenneth W. Thomas and Ralph H. Kilmann, best known for creating a personal conflict style assessment tool, define conflict as a situation in which two or more persons' concerns *appear* to be incompatible and bad feelings may be involved. In conflict, people face the challenge of sorting out what is real and what is only perceived concerning incompatible goals and managing hostile feelings.

Interviews with children reveal that conflict is viewed negatively by young people. A ten-year-old boy defined conflict as follows: "Conflict is when people fight each other and don't agree." Similarly, a sixteen-year-old girl said that conflict involves "two opposing sides against each other and disagreeing." An especially insightful thirteen-year-old boy broadened the definition of conflict to include internal struggles by saying "it could be a disagreement within yourself about something. Like when I'm 21 and could drink alcohol, but I might not want to, so I would be in disagreement with myself." Finally, a young preschooler boy, perhaps focused on securing more playdates, said that conflict "is when your schedules don't match up."

Adults also are familiar with and share many of these negative perceptions about conflict. As one seasoned mother of four children said, "I see conflict as when someone has a set idea in their mind and they are trying to impose that ideal on others or on themselves without a clear plan of how to work together or the motivation to make necessary changes." Although adults often use more sophisticated reasoning, they must move beyond a fear, disdain, or aversion to conflict, as well as differentiate between conflict and contention.

Despite the potential for bad feelings, conflict (defined as differences that matter) does not have to involve bad feelings or become contentious. We may encounter natural "differences" like bumping against another person in a crowd. Yet, contention begins when one or more of the parties involved in the bump expresses hostility or bad feelings toward the other party for the bump. While conflict reflects difference or friction, contention involves the additional layer of negative emotions like anger or hostility.

Workbook Questions:

- How do I define conflict?

- When have I experienced conflict without negative feelings? With negative feelings?

- How do I distinguish a conflict from contention, a disagreement, or a dispute?

Root Causes of Conflict

Most conflict behavior shares the same root cause: perceived or actual incompatible goals between people. *Goal incompatibility simply means that we want, or appear to want, different things.* According to conflict theorists, the late Dr. Otomar J. Bartos and Dr. Paul Wehr of the University of Colorado at Boulder, goal incompatibility stems from three main sources, including:

- *Contested Resources*: We perceive and desire what appears to be a limited amount of such things as money, power, personal time, or prestige.

- *Incompatible Roles*: We play different roles with

potentially imbalanced power positions.

- *Incompatible Values*: We have a different view of the world, which results in wanting different things.

Contested Resources (We Try to Get Our Share of the Pie)

We live in a competitive society where we often perceive that certain desirable resources—like money, quality time, power, prestige, or even affection—are limited. In short, people believe there is only so much pie to divide, so they seek to assertively secure as much of the pie for themselves as they can get. People often behave as if only one pie exists. This pie may represent power, access to privileges, and, perhaps, the ability to produce more pie in the future for our own enjoyment.

Here's an example from a few years ago when I intervened in a dispute between two of my boys over a finite (but large) number of Legos.

One afternoon, my seven-year-old boy, Ethan, was having a temper tantrum because his younger brother, Jack, had destroyed several of his Lego creations. Although Ethan was screaming, my first instinct was to punish Jack for having destroyed Ethan's stuff. But, I took the time to do a little investigating and allowed each boy to tell me his version of what happened and how he felt about it. Ethan was noticeably upset, which made sense to me, but I was surprised to see how angry Jack was. In fact, he could hardly even talk he appeared so angry. I asked him to tell me in words what he was feeling. He finally mustered: "I am really angry at

Ethan." I asked him why, and it took him a while to speak, but he finally blurted out, "Because he thinks all the Legos are his." I then restated what I'd heard him say: "So you're angry with Ethan because he acts like all the Legos are his?"

In our homes, we may experience the battle for contested resources over how to spend our time, money, energy, and even how to divide up the Legos. How do we divide the twenty-four hours available to us each day? As individuals, we must decide how much time and energy we put into relationships with our spouse or partner versus our children or friends. We also must negotiate how much time we spend at work versus participating in our hobbies or being with our families. Our children may jockey for access to our love, time, and special privileges, competing with their siblings for perceived limited parent resources. Like our children, we realize that adults and children must settle issues of contested resources, even if the resources differ in perceived importance and quality.

Our perception that desired resources are limited, or may soon disappear, generates survival instincts even in our youngest children. Likely, we have witnessed our children's competition with each other to secure contested resources at home. As we recognize this fundamental source of conflict, we can examine how we divide the most important finite or disputed resources in our homes, especially time and parent attention.

Workbook Questions:

- What are the contested resources in my life? In my home?

- How do the members of my family compete for limited resources such as time, money, privileges, and parent attention?

- Is there anything I'd like to change now about how I deal with or distribute contested family resources?

Incompatible Roles (Our Roles May Oppose Each Other or Reflect Power Imbalances)

Parents play a variety of roles in their busy lives that reflect their values, responsibilities, goals, and expressions of power. These roles include spouse, parent, child, aunt, trusted friend, coworker, counselor, philanthropist, competitor, and so on. They may bump up against each other in seemingly incompatible or competitive ways that create conflict or contention.

In a basketball game, my role as a player naturally pits me against a player from the other team, but also perhaps a referee from another league. A stay-at-home parent may naturally focus more on responsibilities around the home, while the working parent focuses on relaxing after returning home from work. With two working parents, these caregiving and parenting roles may blend and require a more deliberate division of duties to manage potential conflict that comes from differing, competing, or even similar roles.

In our less hierarchical and looser social structure, the

lack of defined family roles may lead to confusion and unexpressed expectations. Our unspoken expectations about our roles and related responsibilities may lead to patterns and feelings of conflict toward others. Again, even perceived, but not actual, differences about our roles and responsibilities may fuel conflict or the belief in differences between us.

Power Imbalances

Within families, parents and children often play incompatible roles infused with power imbalances. Remember the tension between parent desire for quick reconciliation and child demand for decision-making autonomy? These potentially incompatible roles between parent and child are illustrated by expressions like "I'm the parent, you're the child" or "Listen to me because I know what's best for you." You likely have direct experience with the defiance, defensiveness, or sulking that come from using these tactics with your children.

Asserting parental authority may reveal a very real power imbalance in our children's lives. Interestingly, children may readily learn to imitate parental assertions of power through direct experience over many years. Parents should not be surprised when children replicate our competitive conflict approaches, particularly when they become parents themselves. Children often mirror the conflict approaches parents use with them once they gain increased personal power in their lives.

For example, in sibling conflict, we see power imbalances between children when an older child dominates conflict negotiations with their younger sibling(s). Generally, older siblings enjoy more power in sibling conflicts because they communicate more clearly, have more mature reasoning skills, and are usually bigger in size. (This pattern may reflect the way parents sometimes dominate conflicts with our children using similar assets and associated power tactics.)

We can improve the balance of power between children by supporting the less powerful (i.e., younger, more vulnerable) siblings. As parents, we can help buffer the tendency for our older children to abuse power with their younger siblings by becoming more aware of power differences and by using more constructive resolution processes. However, we need to remain aware that these role differences create potential sources of everyday family conflict between children and parents, and siblings with each other.

As parents, we have more life experience and enjoy greater power and autonomy, especially when it comes to young children. Of course, we want to guide our children toward positive ends. But, if we do not negotiate and attempt to balance these power differences carefully during children's younger years, more intractable power struggles may erupt as our children mature. Even our young children may have something to offer in their roles as children besides obedience to our authority to balance power (and increase role compatibility) in the home.

Parents can be mindful to offer opportunities that balance power differentials in family relationships, even with very young children. Rather than remaining opponents in an imbalanced power situation, we may learn to work side-by-side with our children as joint problem solvers. Furthermore, instead of seeking to solve problems for our children, we can assist them in resolving their own problems, particularly with each other. Like adults, we notice that even very young children desire respect and autonomy in making decisions about their lives.

Workbook Questions:

- What are the main roles you play in your daily life?
- In which roles do you experience role incompatibility?
- How do you handle role incompatibility and/or power differences in your relationships?
- In your family life, which relationships possess equal power differentials?
- How are you trying to balance power differentials in your family life (spousal, parent-child, among siblings)?

Incompatible Values (We Have a Different View of the World, Which Results in Wanting Different Things)

People conflict with each other because they have incompatible values or beliefs as unique individuals with diverse perspectives, attitudes, and behaviors. We may literally see and believe in the worth of opposing values and outcomes. As a parent, you may believe that punk rock is worthless, but your child loves the music and wants to play it loudly in his or her room at night. On the other hand, you may believe that all animals should be treated compassionately, while a loving spouse enjoys hunting as a leisure activity. These examples represent differing values and beliefs, and they are just that: different and often opposing.

We must be wary of our tendency to confuse real with perceived incompatibility in goals and values. Conflicts often erupt because of *perceptions* of incompatible values. In talking with the teenager who loves loud punk rock music, we could find an overlapping interest in enjoying loud, lively music. Even if a particular variation of music doesn't satisfy both the parent and the child, there is some common ground. While more extreme, the hunter and animal rights defender may find a shared love and appreciation of nature, although many areas of difference remain.

Too often, we jump to the conclusion that we are too different in our values or beliefs to try to get along, so we avoid resolving the conflict at all. Unfortunately, instead of seeking collaboration, people try to prove they're right or just avoid potential areas of disagreement. We must be very careful to approach others' values and beliefs with an eye for identifying overlapping or common areas of agreement or belief rather than first assuming difference with others. If we can even imagine the possibility of common ground, we are much more likely to work through any real or perceived value or belief differences we may encounter. We may not always find common ground because our values often do differ. However, we should not prematurely assume our conflict involves opposing values rather than other sources of perceived differences because our interests often do overlap, even if our proposed solutions differ.

Finally, as suggested by conflict theorists and practitioners, Drs. Michael Spangle and Myra Isenhart, even when actual conflicts exist in resources, roles, and values, we may disagree about how to resolve our differences or where to begin discussing them. Consider these areas where further conflict can arrive:

- **Information**: What information do we rely on to make a decision? Do we disagree about what information is correct or what standards are used for judgment?

- **Procedures**: Do we agree on a method to solve a problem, make a decision, or resolve a conflict?

- **Relationships**: Do we trust, respect, and believe in the honesty of the other person?

- **Communication**: Did we phrase our conflict, problem, or question to avoid creating more contention and defensiveness in others?

Given our potential to disagree about what information counts, what procedures should be used for decision-making, relative relationship trust, and our preferred communication patterns, we should carefully consider the pros and cons of various conflict approaches. Ideally, we outline what information counts, what procedure will be used, and what manner of communication is expected before conflict occurs in specific contexts within our lives. In chapter 10, I talk about the importance of family meetings and establishing family rules to guide our decisions about information, procedures, relationships, and communication to prevent and avoid unnecessary conflict at home.

Workbook Questions:

- Whom do I have regular conflicts with over incompatible values?

- Is there an overlap of values despite my perception of incompatibility? If so, where is the overlap?

- How do information, procedures, relationship trust, and communication preferences play into conflicts that I have experienced or am experiencing now?

Addressing Individual Areas of Mental or Physical Health Affecting Conflict Patterns

In discussing conflict, we naturally consider key behaviors and circumstances that drive conflict, including addiction, mental or physical pain or illness, hunger, thirst, fatigue, and stress. We know that when we have unmet needs, or we are abusing ourselves or others, we often live in a state of conflict regardless of other people's behavior. Our addictions, guilt, stress, hunger, physical or mental illnesses, and other personal adversities may dramatically affect our ability to deal with conflict constructively and actually may fuel conflict.

We must address these personal problems before (or at least while) we hope to change our interactions with others.

For example, perfectionism may lead to many types of conflict behaviors that have little to do with the other person's behavior.

One of my sons takes piano lessons. Several years ago, for the third lesson in a row, my son's behavior toward his kind, gentle piano teacher changed. My son was struggling with a song, and each time he made a mistake, he started over from the beginning. After three attempts, my son grew enraged, pounding the piano and trying to crumple the piano music. He ran to his room, ending the piano lesson. Once my husband got home, he spoke one-on-one with our son to figure out what was going on. He told my husband that he likes piano, which seemed contrary to his behavior earlier in the day. The real problem, he explained, was not being able to play the song perfectly.

Each week, he kept getting harder and harder songs that he didn't know, so he felt imperfect and anxious each time the piano teacher arrived. In this case, my son's conflict was with himself, though it appeared that it was a problem with his piano teacher. His frustration with imperfection created an internal conflict. Knowing this, my husband and I are learning to help him work through his feelings because, as he says, he really does like piano.

If you or your child experience significant personal challenges, like addiction, physical or mental illness, or even extreme stress, I challenge you to actively address your issues.

Seek the individual help required, perhaps by trained professionals who can help you resolve the inner struggles that deeply affect your social interactions, particularly at home, work, and school. Finding a solution can make a huge difference. In my own home, we learned that a significant food allergy was causing another son's distress in different areas of his life. Rather than focusing on his behavior toward others, we shifted our attention to the root cause. Once we resolved this outstanding health issue, our son's interactions with his siblings and others significantly improved.

Workbook Questions:

- Do I have any outstanding personal issues that are fueling conflicts in my personal life?

- If so, what are those personal issues? How can I resolve these personal issues?

- What are some personal habits, challenges, or illnesses of mine (or of my children) that may be affecting the conflict climate in my home?

- How am I addressing these negative personal habits or situations to improve my home atmosphere?

Societal Trends in Conflict and Conflict Management

We now have easy access to information about disturbing real-time national and international conflicts. We are inundated with images of seemingly intractable conflicts, including war, terrorism, and abuse. While we may feel obligated to stay informed about world events, we often feel powerless to influence conflict positively in far-away places.

Accept Violence as Entertainment and Disregard Social Priming for Violent Conflict Behavior

Despite feeling troubled by real wars, terrorism, and other violent conflicts around the world, in Western culture, we consume mass quantities of violence in the form of entertainment. In short, we experience angst over depressing news on CNN, but choose violent movies, music, video games, books, and magazines for personal pleasure. While we try to limit the amount of violent entertainment our kids experience in our home, I have learned that even a little can be too much.

One night, my husband and I returned home from a date to hear my daughter's report that my two older boys had been fighting. Our oldest daughter said she had no idea what they'd been fighting about, but had heard one boy scream and saw him leave his older brother behind in the basement. After asking our younger son several questions before bedtime, I finally got a decent version of the "fight." Very hesitantly, my son revealed to me that a big physical fight erupted when they were trying to imitate Pokémon characters.

My husband and I had already discussed how violent media primes people for violent behavior, but I had deemed it fairly harmless for the boys to watch one episode of Pokémon a day. In our house, we have all kinds of wrestling and tumbling among the boys on a regular basis, but this particular type of fighting to hurt the other person felt different. When I heard my young son's explanation, I quickly realized that even in a small way, I had knowingly facilitated aggressive behavior by providing violent priming media to my young, energetic sons.

Avoid or Inappropriately Escalate Everyday Conflict Situations

Beyond watching violent media as entertainment, we feel uncomfortable dealing with the more mundane experiences of personal conflict in our everyday lives. We often don't constructively resolve our personal conflicts at all. Instead of resolving a conflict with a loved one, people run from the conflict by drinking excessively, gossiping, punishing a loved one with the silent treatment, or even moving thousands of miles away to extinguish the possibility of contact.

On the flip side of avoidance, people overreact to and escalate normal conflict situations. Imagine one neighbor can no longer stand another neighbor's dog barking at night. Instead of talking things over, the upset neighbor might call the cops to resolve the issue for them. In this case, they have turned a small annoyance in daily life into a situation requiring the involvement of police officers. Calling in the big guns might escalate rather than de-escalate the conflict situation. Indeed, this way of managing the conflict creates a larger conflict out of a potentially small issue that could be talked through reasonably given the appropriate framework and

In different areas of life, people see themselves and others overreacting, underreacting, and sometimes not reacting at all to conflict situations that matter to both individuals and communities. By not effectively resolving conflict, people not only risk losing or weakening valuable relationships, but we also set ourselves up for occasional conflict explosions.

Treat Conflict with Urgent Rather Than Preventive Care

In addition to escalating small conflicts into volatile situations requiring professional intervention, people often treat conflict management in their personal and professional lives much like they do their health; we tend to avoid preventive medicine in favor of the urgent care approach. They wait until a conflict becomes a problem needing professional assistance (think about the barking dog example). In short, people avoid resolving ordinary conflict before it blossoms into full-grown contentions that they feel unable to resolve themselves.

People rely on others to resolve daily conflicts and allow them to grow until they need outside assistance. They allow mole hills of conflict to grow into mountains of contention because they avoid constructively dealing with the everyday issues. In essence, people seek help when they can no longer avoid conflicts because they have lost control of situations.

Understanding How our Social Institutions Deal with Conflict

Our institutions do not often provide a means to resolve differences without outside help. If we look closely, many of our social institutions, like schools, churches, rec centers, and many places of employment do not provide for the reconciliation of differences without outside assistance. Instead, they rely on intervention from HR professionals, police officers, lawyers, and other highly specialized paid professionals once conflicts have grown into truly contentious issues. Certainly, in heated conflict situations, people call on lawyers, courts, juries, policemen, security officers, and government officials to guide them through conflict situations.

In fact, society is primarily set up in a way to avoid dealing with everyday conflicts. While alternative dispute resolution practices have gained footing in some areas of society, most institutions still rely heavily on the court system, which rarely involves personal reconciliation between parties in conflict.

Through the court system, the parties pay awards or penalties for wrongs rather than offer apologies, increased communication, and restitution following conflict episodes. Patterns at home often reflect larger societal patterns influenced by the adversarial nature of our court system. How would schools, work places, and, particularly, home life be improved if people assumed the ongoing need for conflict resolution, rather than expecting conflicts to disappear on their own or be managed by a higher authority? Could people try to soothe feelings and resolve misunderstandings before they become so large that they require a court, judge, and jury for resolution?

In this complex, highly competitive society that manages to flex under the strain of diverse conflicts, we can see the effects of inadequate conflict management both at the macro levels of global government and in the private quarters of the home. The foundation of any society is based on the beliefs and actions of its individual citizens. In short, if we can learn to be at peace with ourselves and with our families on the micro level, that positive influence will spread throughout society at large.

The Differences between Constructive and Destructive Conflict Patterns

Before moving on to the next chapter, I wrap up this section by outlining both constructive and destructive conflict outcomes and approaches in our lives. While some level of conflict is normal and natural in life, some forms of conflict prevent or damage our growth, development, and well-being, as well as our children's.

Given how easy it is to deal with conflict unsuccessfully, in this book, I focus on how to manage conflict effectively and constructively in family life. As parents, we focus on developing the communication skills that are essential to all human relationships throughout our lifetime. Once we've trained ourselves, we become ready to begin teaching and modeling effective conflict management patterns to our children.

As the basic social institution in society, our families may benefit from learning from research about both constructive and destructive conflict management patterns. From conflict theorists Dr. Morton Deutsch, Dr. Michael Spangle, and Dr. Myra Isenhart, we learn that in negative conflict situations, opposing parties express strong, hostile emotions and often try to control others using power differences. You can recognize destructive conflict management patterns when people in conflicting groups demonstrate the following behaviors:

- Express strong negative emotions such as anger, jealousy, frustration, and intolerance

- Refuse to hear others' ideas and automatically reject others' input

- Interrupt others or do not allow others to speak

- Distract from the main topic of discussion

- Attempt to create greater differences among people

- Identify clear winners and losers in the decision-making process

- Try to make themselves more powerful than others

- Use negative stereotyping or name-calling when referring to conflict parties

- Shift toward group conformity or forcing the group to think and behave similarly

Workbook Questions:

- When do I fall into negative conflict patterns?

- Do I know why I follow or exhibit these negative patterns of behavior in certain situations?

- When have I been involved in a group conflict situation that deteriorated because of negative conflict patterns? If so, how would I describe the negative processes at work?

Constructive conflict patterns *center on the issues, ideas, and tasks* within a cooperative or collaborative framework. People who use constructive approaches to conflict may do the following:

- Encourage exploring new approaches and ways of looking at a problem
- Express friendliness and helpfulness to others in the group
- Share or build power in others without feeling threatened
- Define conflicting interests as a joint problem to be solved
- Increase the group's commitment to the organization
- Strengthen creative processes by being open to new ideas
- Cultivate trust so that others feel comfortable sharing ideas and brainstorming solutions

Workbook Questions:

- When have I been involved in a group that used positive conflict patterns? If so, how would I describe how the conflict led to positive results for the group?
- Describe a positive group conflict experience I have seen with my family.

Naturally, many of us resist dealing with conflict up front, but constructive management of conflict may help us and our children grow in our understanding and intimacy with each other. As we begin to consciously understand the sources of our personal conflict and that of our children, we are better equipped to then learn how to channel conflict situations through effective processes.

In the following chapter, I focus on how you can become consciously aware of your usual ways for dealing with conflict and explore the five general conflict approaches. From avoiding to collaborating, I discuss the pros and cons and ideal conditions for each of the five conflict approaches. Continuing in chapters 2 through 7, you will explore topics such as child development milestones related to conflict resolution, the sibling relationship, and sibling conflict. These upcoming five chapters build the foundation for chapter 8, which introduces the formal principles of parent-led mediation.

Chapter 1 Summary

Definition of Conflict

A situation in which two or more people's concerns *appear* to be incompatible and bad feelings may be involved.

The Feelings of Conflict/Contention

While we may have clear identification of the feelings involved in conflict, we benefit from understanding the thoughts driving conflict. In addition, we investigate both the behaviors and feelings associated with conflict.

Drivers of Conflict

Most conflicts arise from perceived or real incompatible goals or feelings of hostility. Perceived or real incompatible goals are influenced by our perceptions of and experiences with the following:

- *Contested Resources:* We perceive and desire such things as money, power, personal time, or prestige, which appear to be limited.
- *Incompatible Roles*: We play different roles with potential imbalances in power positions.
- *Incompatible Values:* We have a different view of the

world, which results in wanting different things.
In addition, we may have disagreements about conflict resolution procedures:

- *Information* (standards, criteria): What information do we rely on to make a decision? Do we disagree about what information is correct or what standards are used for judgment?

- *Procedures*: Do we agree on a method to solve a problem, make a decision, or resolve a conflict?

- *Relationships*: Is there trust, respect, and a belief in the honesty of the opposing party?

- *Communication*: Did we phrase our conflict, problem, or question in a way that avoids misunderstandings?

Understanding Cultural Patterns of and Assumptions about Conflict

- *Priming for Violence through Media*: As a culture, we accept violence as entertainment and lack the skills needed to resolve our daily conflicts.

- *Urgent vs. Preventive Care*: We often wait until a small problem has grown large before we seek to resolve it.

- *Understanding How Our Social Institutions Deal with Conflict:* Most social institutions in our society are not equipped with adequate conflict resolution practices and processes outside of the legal system. In our homes, we benefit from coming up with a plan for managing regular conflict.

Differentiating between Constructive and Destructive Conflict

- *Constructive Conflict*
  - Focuses on interests, ideas, and tasks
  - Generates discovery and creativity, seeks to enhance the power of others, improves decision-making, and strengthens commitment to an organization if parties trust each other
- *Destructive Conflict*
  - Focuses on people and emotions to assert domination
  - Generates winners and losers, undermines group cohesion, and involves parties criticizing others' ideas, with some seeking to dominate the group, as well as includes a gravitation toward group conformity

CHAPTER 2

FIVE GENERAL APPROACHES TO CONFLICT MANAGEMENT

To teach constructive conflict management to your children effectively, you must first learn and understand how you manage conflict. Consider the following questions: How do you respond to a screaming child? What about an angry boss, a car accident, or a glass of spilled milk? Would you describe yourself as an avoider, a competitor, or a great compromiser?

Your first step is to become aware of your own tendencies and patterns in conflict, which helps you deal with your own conflicts with your children and others, and which your children observe regularly. Once you see your tendencies and patterns, you are prepared to teach your children more constructive ways of dealing with the conflicts they encounter. In a way, your responses to conflict are like separate languages—each with its own expressions, gestures, tone of voice, actions (or even inaction)—used to communicate your goals or interests. As metaphorical linguists, you travel through foreign lands and may need a variety of languages or approaches to effectively communicate with even the same person on different occasions. Your language, or choice of approach, depends on the conflict situation and not just the person.

Every day, parents encounter different kinds of minor to major conflicts that challenge their ability to respond constructively and flexibly. From experience, you know that no single approach to conflict will work in every situation, even with the people you interact with every day. Instead, you adapt your conflict approach to the specific conditions and needs you encounter.

While hundreds of foreign languages and dialects exist, there are five main approaches people use to deal with conflict. These conflict management approaches include avoiding, accommodating, competing, compromising, and collaborating. By becoming skilled in each of these approaches, you can learn to more effectively communicate and resolve conflict in ways tailored to certain people, situations, and your respective goals.

Exploring Our Native Conflict Approaches

Each person is born with a general disposition, but our preferred conflict approaches are also heavily influenced by how we were raised, including our unique culture, school or work experience, peer groups, and, most importantly, our families.

From a very early age, through the words and actions of others, we begin learning patterns of social behavior to guide our actions in a variety of social settings. Depending upon the circumstance, we may learn to compromise quickly on the playground by sharing one of two swings with our peers, but fight tooth and nail with a close sibling over who gets to swing on the one swing in the backyard. In short, as we do with native languages, we learn both direct and unstated rules about how to express and work through conflict situations at home, school, with peers, and so on.

According to mediators, Dr. Jennifer E. Beer and Eileen Stief, who wrote *The Mediator's Handbook*, there are three elements in all conflict approaches, which address these elements in different ways:

- <u>People</u> (relationships and personalities)
- <u>Process</u> (the way that people respond to conflict can intensify, ease, or spread conflict)
- <u>Problem</u> (the issues or interests that causes conflict to arise)

Learning New Languages

To become skilled in conflict resolution, one key is to gain an awareness of your "native" conflict language(s) first. By native conflict language, I mean how people generally approach conflict, their thoughts, emotions, words, behaviors, gestures, and reactions, both large and small. I say *native* because it implies a sense of instinct or habit that comes from an automatic or unconscious reaction. People learn conflict approaches, which heavily influence how they deal with daily conflict in both constructive and destructive ways, from a

47

very young age based on how they were raised and their given temperaments.

Rather than thinking of approaches and reactions to conflict solely as a facet of personality, consider that they are more like a learned language than a fixed genetic trait. Parents and other caregivers are the primary teachers of conflict management for children. They imitate both the positive and negative approaches they observe, just like they imitate the words parents say and the tones of voice they hear. Beyond mere words and intonation, children learn to imitate conflict approaches, including the use of active listening, which means that a listener fully concentrates, understands, responds, and then remembers what is being said. In addition, children learn to imitate others' expression or lack of empathy, physical or verbal aggression, perspective taking, allowance for freedom of expression, or laying down of judgments or punishments.

As you attempt to identify, define, and assess different approaches to conflict, keep in mind that each approach addresses people, process, and problems in different ways. Some strategies are more effective than others given your goals and interests in the moment.

Workbook Questions:

- How do I usually approach conflict with my spouse or partner?
- How do I usually approach conflict with my coworkers?
- How do I usually approach conflict with my children?

- If there are differences in my approaches, how are they different, and why?

Five Main Conflict Approaches

Identification of the Conflict Approaches by Essential Characteristics

Many different methods exist to resolve conflict, but we use five main approaches. The five conflict approaches reflect different degrees of assertiveness (in other words, meeting our own goals) and cooperativeness (meeting others' goals). Each general approach represents goals and values and involves benefits and drawbacks depending upon the purpose for selecting that approach.

Assertiveness and cooperativeness are not meant to be considered in terms of good or bad, but as a focus on your personal goals or the goals of others. There are different times, seasons, and situations to prioritize personal goals, others' goals, and both parties' goals. The key is to know when to use the conflict strategy appropriately.

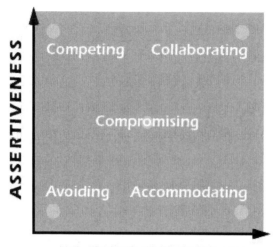

COOPERATIVENESS

For simplicity, I use the terms and ideas coined by conflict theorists, Kenneth W. Thomas and Ralph H. Kilmann, who are best known for creating a personal conflict style assessment. The five main conflict approaches include the following:

- Avoiding
- Accommodating
- Compromising
- Competing
- Collaborating

The graphic on page 50 presents the five conflict approaches along the range of seeking to satisfy our own goals (assertiveness) and seeking to satisfy other people's goals (cooperativeness).

In this next section, I explore fuller definitions, meanings, and pros and cons of each of the five general conflict approaches based on the ideas and research of Thomas and Kilmann, as well as Drs. Michael Spangle and Myra Isenhart, conflict resolution academics and practitioners.

Rather than focus on learning a new conflict approach or justifying the use of a certain strategy, the best course is to learn each of the five approaches. You want to know all of them well enough to be able to apply them in the right situations to satisfy your own and others' goals. The intention is to grasp each approach's usefulness in the diverse conflict situations you encounter in your daily life.

Definition of Each Conflict Approach

The working definitions I use are paraphrased from conflict specialists Spangle and Isenhart.

- **Avoiding**

  One party denies that a conflict exists, changes the subject, or avoids discussion and is noncommittal (no one wins or loses in the moment).

- **Accommodating**

  One party sacrifices his or her interests and concerns

while enabling others to achieve their interests (you win and I lose).

- **Compromising**
  Through concessions by all parties, everyone accepts partial satisfaction of their interests (both win and both lose in certain ways).

- **Competing**
  One party is aggressive, self-focused, forcing, verbally assertive, and uncooperative to satisfy his or her own interests at the expense of the interests of others (win-lose orientation).

- **Collaborating**
  Parties use active listening and issue-focused, empathic communication to satisfy the interests and concerns of all parties (win-win orientation).

Potential Goals or Meaning Behind Each Conflict Language

Different approaches work in different situations. Just as using German with the English-speaking cashier at your local grocery store might not allow for real communication, collaborating won't always be appropriate, especially in forceful, competitive negotiations in the workplace. No single method will be appropriate for every conflict situation you encounter.

Throughout a lifetime, becoming fluent in each of the five approaches allows you to achieve your own interests and goals in each situation. While all people benefit from learning and applying all the conflict approaches appropriately, parents may need to shift gears more quickly and employ multiple approaches at the same time because of the different abilities of their children.

For example, after driving a hard negotiation with a potential buyer at work, can I return home and switch my tactic to accommodating or collaborating if my tired toddler refuses to eat the meal that I have prepared? Will I be prepared to avoid talking with the solicitor who knocks on my door while I'm eating dinner with my family? Later that evening, can I then carefully listen to my partner vent his or her frustration about a distressing health issue without tuning out or trying to solve the problem myself?

Each relationship and situation may demand some flexibility and insight to get the right balance of achieving your own goals and others'. With your increased awareness and understanding of the five approaches, you will enhance the possibility of reaching your diverse goals and interests. You are not too old to learn new approaches and teach your children communication skills beyond their current habits and abilities.

Pros and Cons of Each Conflict Approach and Best Conditions for Use

Given that we all have native tendencies and habitual conflict approaches, we may over-, under-, or misuse certain conflict approaches in our lives. In this section, I share the pros and cons of each of the five conflict approaches so you can better understand how each one could help or hinder you in reaching your communication and relationship goals with each other.

Although it's difficult to predict the particulars of each conflict situation you might encounter, it's helpful to understand the ideal situations and conditions for each conflict approach. I briefly highlight the contexts most suited to reaching certain goals using specific conflict management approaches to help you develop your own decision-making compass or framework for conflict.

Following a description of the goals, pros and cons, and ideal conditions for each approach, you will find several workbook questions to help you examine how familiar you are with and how often you use each conflict approach in your life. These questions are most useful when you reflect on your personal conflict management habits in different relationships, and not only when parenting.

AVOIDING

Avoiding, or not seeking to address a conflict, is used to maintain current conditions or a sense of balance with yourself and others. This approach may help you avoid humiliating yourself or others in tense or socially awkward situations. In addition, avoiding may serve to release tension in unfamiliar or uncomfortable situations. Sometimes you may need extra time to reflect before responding to a tense or otherwise undesirable situation, especially when you are unsure of how to respond effectively.

- Pros: You may reduce the risk of physical or mental abuse and decrease immediate stress in situations that are out of your control or that you don't consider important. This approach may give you time for reflection or demonstrate compassion for someone who is not ready to confront a conflict head-on.

- Cons: Regular avoidance in your close relationships creates the risk of failing to reflect or satisfy your needs and desires. Avoiding may also isolate you from others rather than provide the stability and social connection you seek.

- Ideal Conditions: Avoiding is most useful when (1) you are involved in a potentially dangerous situation involving physical violence, (2) the issue is not important to you, (3) there is no chance of achieving your goals, or (4) the complexity of the situation prevents solutions.

Workbook Questions:

- When do I avoid conflict?

- How does avoiding usually work for me?

- In which situations would avoiding help me reach my goals or interests?

- In which situations should I try a different method besides avoiding?

ACCOMMODATING

When we accommodate, we give up something we want so that others can achieve their goals. People often accommodate others to prevent an unnecessary confrontation or to maintain harmony in an awkward or potentially volatile social situation. If your goal is to appear generous or gracious in a variety of social situations, accommodating can help. This approach may also preserve your own and others' dignity. Finally, accommodating may serve as a sign of deference to an authority figure or to the position of another powerful or important person.

- Pros: With accommodating, you may be seeking to maintain a sense of harmony or "peace" with others. This approach may also confirm to others that you are a generous, caring person who is concerned about others. Accommodating is considered mandatory in certain social settings, like the workplace and government.

- Cons: Just as with avoiding, when you accommodate, you may not be taking into account your own needs and desires and communicating them. This approach may alienate you in your intimate relationships if you do not balance both your personal and cooperative needs and goals.

- Ideal Conditions: Accommodating is effective in situations when (1) there is not much chance of achieving your interests, (2) the outcomes are not important, or (3) you believe that satisfying your interests will in some way alter or damage a relationship.

Workbook Questions:

- When do I accommodate others in conflict?
- What kinds of outcomes do I expect when I use this approach?
- What kinds of outcomes do I usually achieve when I accommodate?
- Are there situations in my life where I am accommodating too much or too little? If so, what approach would be more effective?

COMPROMISING

At the center of the diagram sits compromise, representing meeting personal needs and satisfying others' needs. This popular approach may help you settle a conflict quickly in a socially acceptable way. Compromising can be used to avoid a tricky or overly tense situation with some form of "let's split the difference." This approach provides the appearance of fairness when people fight and sets a precedent for future conflicts with similar conditions. Finally, compromising can demonstrate self-confidence while respecting others' goals and interests.

To understand the go-to conflict resolution method in Western culture, imagine that two people are trying to decide what to do with an orange. One person wants the peel to grate for orange zest when the recipe calls for the whole orange, and the other person is hungry enough to eat the entire fruit. As a compromise, the two people may split the orange in two, providing each person with only half of what they had originally wanted: either all the peel or all the orange pieces inside.

Despite its popularity and ease of use, compromising may not always get you what you want. Both people could lose, in a sense, by securing only half of the peel and half of the orange slices. It is important to remember that compromising sometimes is a "lose-lose" method in our family lives. Often, parents overuse compromise to settle disputes over fairness and family privileges that warrant another approach, especially collaboration.

- Pros: Compromising is considered a fast, efficient, and culturally acceptable way to deal with conflict. This approach is easily understood and applied by most people in Western culture.

- Cons: With compromise, each party in a conflict must give up something for resolution, so it is lose-lose in that sense. Compromise may not get you what you desire—perhaps, only part of what you want. This approach may also reflect our inability to connect on a deeper level over difficult issues, masking greater issues that need true resolution.

- Ideal Conditions: This approach is effective in situations when (1) quick resolution of issues is needed, (2) parties opposing us resist collaboration, (3) complete achievement of your goals is not important, or (4) there will be no hard feelings between the parties for settling for less than expected.

Workbook Questions:

- When am I most likely to compromise?
- How do I feel about the compromises I make?
- Would I like to change anything about what I compromise on or with whom I compromise?
- What situations in my life seem most appropriate for compromising?

COMPETING

When competing, people actively seek to reach their own personal goals. Often, with a competitive approach, you demonstrate your power and/or abilities to achieve your personal goals. Likewise, you may want to set a tone for domination or authority to establish power relationships. At times, you may try to instill fear in the other party to preserve stability and harmony in current and future social situations.

- Pros: With competing, you might get what you want quickly if you don't care about other people's feelings or you need to demonstrate your commitment to a certain position. This approach may help you establish dominance in a social setting.

- Cons: If we use a competitive approach too regularly in our most important, intimate relationships,

· 59

this may result in resentment and defiance. When we use force to realize our personal goals, we may permanently damage a working or more intimate relationship.

- Ideal Conditions: This style is effective in situations when (1) we need to make decisions quickly, (2) our options are restricted, (3) there is nothing to lose by pushing, (4) other parties resist cooperation, and (5) there is no concern about potential damage to the relationship.

Workbook Questions:

- When do I compete with others to resolve conflict?
- What has been my experience with using competition to resolve conflict at work, home, and in the community?
- In what areas of my life could I benefit from using a competitive approach to conflict?
- In what areas of my life could I benefit from using an approach other than competing?

COLLABORATING

When you collaborate, you demonstrate a commitment to the relationship with careful use of time, energy, and listening. Collaborating helps you build trust and conveys your empathy and a willingness to listen while maintaining a balance between both personal and other-focused goals.

Generally, collaborating represents a more balanced approach than giving in to someone else's goals or demanding that another person or party give in to your wishes.

- <u>Pros</u>: Collaborative approaches help you to build relationships with important others and creates win-win outcomes. Collaborating helps to balance power differentials and demonstrate respect and appreciation for each party's value. This approach expands creativity and imagination and often results in innovative solutions.

- <u>Cons</u>: Collaborating is fairly time-consuming and not always worth the effort for insignificant issues. To be effective in collaborating, both parties need a certain level of trust in each other's sincerity and possess a proficiency with certain communication skills (for example, active listening, reframing, and constructive questioning).

- <u>Ideal Conditions</u>: Collaborating is effective in situations when (1) power is reasonably balanced, (2) you value the long-term relationship, (3) both parties display cooperative behaviors, (4) and there is sufficient time and energy to create a win-win solution that satisfies both sides.

Workbook Questions:

- When do I collaborate with others to resolve conflict?
- What has been my experience with collaborating?

- How effective do I feel I am with collaborating?

- Who do I collaborate with well? Who do I have difficulty collaborating with? Why?

Challenges to Effective Conflict Communication

Even with this framework of five conflict approaches in mind, you could face many types of miscommunications each day. According to communications expert Nick Perrin, in daily life people miscommunicate with each other in three basic ways:

1. <u>Misunderstanding</u>: A receiver understands the message differently than what the sender intended. For example, one advertisement read: "Illiterate? Write today for help."

2. <u>Non-Understanding</u>: The message receiver receives no message at all due to hearing loss, a bad connection, or a language barrier. For example, if my cell phone connection were limited and I could not make out what you were saying.

3. <u>Misinterpretation</u>: A message receiver interprets the message differently than the message sender intended due to differing understanding of the words, terms, values, or beliefs. For example, Perrin cites a dry-cleaning shop sign that reads: "Drop your trousers here for best results."

Given the diversity of personalities, experiences, and cultures in the world, we should not be surprised that we experience many types of miscommunications, even within our families. Naturally, we will sometimes misunderstand, not understand at all, or misinterpret the messages people try to communicate with us.

Language Barriers and "Faux Pas"

Like walking into a café in Paris and asking for the menu in English, when you use a specific language in the wrong context, you could receive a negative response, not satisfying either your own or the others person's goals for a social interaction. Often, people experience the strain of a faux pas, but don't know how to behave otherwise. As you gain new skills and communication tools, you experience less discomfort and more real connection with the people you encounter, whether a family member at home or a stranger on the street.

You may apply different approaches to deal with your own conflicts than when trying to resolve others' conflicts. You may learn and apply certain approaches at home, others at school, and still others while interacting at work. As truly adaptable beings, we adjust ourselves to certain conditions and learn patterns that help us better resolve both daily mundane and the more pressing challenges we face in satisfying both individual and collective goals.

Using the Wrong Approach Despite Sincere Intent

Each of us experiences the inner world of personal intent, but may or may not effectively express that intent to other people in a way they can understand. Oftentimes, we react by instinct, reverting to innate patterns governed largely by emotion. We may not be fully aware of why we react the way we do, but with conscious awareness, time, and effort, we can change our patterns.

In my marriage, I've noticed how I sometimes enter a conversation with the intent to collaborate and listen carefully to my husband, but something about his defensive response triggers my avoidance and ultimate rejection of the opportunity to work out a difference between us. For example, when I ask him to listen to me, but he doesn't ask me any questions or share any personal thoughts, I realize that while I asked for listening, I really wanted connection through thoughtful questions and sharing from his side also. What began with a desire to connect may end with a weakening of ties because I didn't convey my message in a way that he could understand. The basics of communication—a sender sends a message and a receiver receives and understands the message—may not have occurred.

When a miscommunication like this happens, I may be incorrectly presenting my intent to collaborate or possibly misunderstanding his intent to collaborate back with me. Miscommunication is common between men and women because we often rely on different social cues and frames of reference! How natural to experience these communication conflicts with our own children, and for our children to experience this with each other!

Recognizing Ineffective Patterns from our Native Conflict Approaches

From parents, friends, employers, peers, and others, people learn effective and ineffective ways of assertively satisfying individual goals and cooperatively helping others achieve their own desires.

Specifically, from my childhood into adulthood, I believed that by primarily avoiding and accommodating others in conflict situations, I would enjoy the emotional intimacy I craved. In essence, I tried to be resiliently peaceful with others and stifle my own desires to be loved. Only during my early forties have I begun to realize that when I don't address important, reoccurring issues with my loved ones, I don't gain the emotional intimacy I seek.

Now, as I have accepted how over-relying on avoiding and accommodating strategies have failed to provide emotional intimacy in my closest relationships, I have begun my quest to not run from, but embrace the opportunities that conflict situations provide for me and my loved ones to grow in understanding and intimacy with each other. I want to pass on a wider range of skills with conflict management to my children so that they may enjoy fuller, more satisfying relationships throughout their lives.

Contrasting with my need for emotional intimacy found through collaboration and sharing, I am also learning to approach conflict competitively when I need to. For example, as I prepared myself to purchase a new car last year, I geared myself up to be openly competitive with, but still courteous to, my salesperson. I researched my options well before stepping into the dealership with a clear understanding that my salesperson desired to obtain the highest price, while I desired the lowest price for a car. I prepped myself with tools from the competitive conflict language landscape so that somehow my salesperson and I could arrive at the right price for the purchase of my car. While not characteristic of my native temperament, I am learning to be competitive in similarly competitive situations to ensure that my needs and goals are met satisfactorily. Sometimes trying out new conflict approaches, especially more assertive ones, with strangers helps decrease the emotional risk we may take.

Indeed, conflict occurs with those both in and outside of our most intimate circle of relationships in a variety of situations. Thus, each conflict situation provides a different opportunity and may require different strategies to help us achieve our particular goals.

Workbook Questions:

- When do I run into roadblocks with being understood during conflicts?

- Who is someone I would like to communicate with more smoothly, but struggle to reach effectively?

- How reflective am I about my approaches to conflict?

- What could I change or improve about my attitude toward conflict?

Becoming Fluent in Conflict Approaches

Anyone can expand their skills and understanding of conflict resolution approaches to suit both the familiar and new conflict situations they encounter. Like trying out foreign languages in a real-life context, you can learn to apply new conflict approaches in appropriate situations through study and by trial and error. You won't succeed in resolving conflict every time, but you will make progress as you practice.

Throughout a lifetime, you can develop *conflict fluency*, which means you're able to skillfully use various conflict approaches in appropriate contexts to achieve your social goals. You do not gain conflict language fluency all at once, but learn through study, preparation, and direct practice. As you become fluent with conflict, your tendencies will become instinctual, and you will naturally identify appropriate responses based on your goals. You can consciously evaluate a situation and identify your needs so that you are less reactive and more proactive in responding to conflict situations when they first occur.

Conclusion

I've shown you how each conflict approach represents different meanings and potentially divergent goals. As with foreign languages, different conflict approaches will help you to meet varying personal and other-focused goals.

Now you know the basic framework of the five conflict approaches and some fundamentals about conflict origins. With this understanding in mind, I now turn to exploring how people learn their current conflict behavior as children, and how you can expand your understanding toward and response to conflict as adults. The next chapter ends with real-life examples of managing various conflicts in my home with combinations of the five general conflict approaches.

Chapter 2 Summary

Definition of Each General Conflict Approach

- **Avoiding**

  One party denies that a conflict exists, changes the subject, or avoids discussion and is noncommittal (no one wins or loses in the moment).

- **Accommodating**

  One party sacrifices his or her interests and concerns while enabling others to achieve their interests (you win and I lose).

- **Compromising**

  Through concessions by all parties, everyone accepts partial satisfaction of their interests (both win and both lose in certain ways).

- **Competing**

  One party is aggressive, self-focused, forcing, verbally assertive, and uncooperative to satisfy his or her own interests at the expense of the interests of others (win-lose orientation).

- **Collaborating**

  Parties use active listening and issue-focused,

empathic communication to satisfy the interests and concerns of all parties (win-win orientation).

Challenges to Effective Conflict Communication

- Language barriers and "faux pas"
- Using the wrong language despite sincere intent
- Recognizing ineffective patterns from our native conflict tongues

Becoming Multilingual (and Fluent) in Conflict Languages

- *Conflict Fluency*: The ability to skillfully use various conflict approaches in appropriate contexts to achieve social goals.

CHAPTER 3

LEARNING CONFLICT APPROACHES AS CHILDREN & ADULTS

As we've discussed, when people learn English in their homes growing up, speaking the language feels natural and even instinctual. Through direct training, observation, and by imitation of others' behavior, parents have developed different approaches to conflict. Parent's conflict management responses are often unconsciously driven after years of practice from early childhood. Our parental conflict responses may seem more difficult to change, but they are still modifiable.

While parents can change conflict habits through diligent effort and practice, children have the benefit of flexible brain structures that allow for easy learning of constructive conflict habits from their earliest days. As parents, we can take advantage of our children's ease with learning by teaching and modeling constructive conflict management habits with our very young children.

Learning Conflict Approaches as a Child

As a young child, I recall vivid experiences learning French as a second language first by imitation. When called upon, I could easily repeat "Comment allez-vous?" without a trace of an American accent. I could easily parrot my teacher's words and pronunciation even though I did not understand what I was saying. Like most children, it was easy to imitate the sounds without even understanding the meaning of the words; my brain through my ears picked up the pronunciation nuances, and the mouth repeated back what I'd heard. I didn't understand the mechanics of it, but I could imitate the desired behavior.

Children Learn to Imitate Role Models'
Communication Patterns

Some skills and habits, especially language and other communication skills, seem (and are) easier to learn in childhood and become almost instinctual or beyond conscious awareness. During elementary school, I gained an eventual awareness that other languages existed beyond English and that I could learn to communicate with others using new languages. These early experiences of gaining an awareness of different approaches to the spoken language have helped me understand that conflict approaches are also both learned and learnable even into adulthood.

Children learn to communicate by first imitating both the good and the bad skills and behaviors of important adults in their lives, such as parents, teachers, and other mentors.

Just as people sometimes adopt improper grammar or speak with a limited vocabulary, people also learn some ineffective conflict resolution philosophies and methods that do not support their goals and aspirations. Children do not necessarily have a good communication/bad communication filter that allows them to weed out the negative patterns they have learned. As you work to learn more about the different approaches, you might discover (or may have already discovered) that some approaches you use in certain circumstances don't serve you.

Workbook Questions:

- How did I learn certain conflict approaches as a child?

- As a child, who served as positive examples of conflict management in my life? What did I learn from how they dealt with conflict?

- As a child, who served as negative examples of conflict management in my life? What did I learn from how they dealt with conflict?

- Where did I learn to avoid? Accommodate? Compromise? Compete? Collaborate?

Learning New Approaches as Adults

The approaches people use most often may feel instinctual—as if they're just part of our personality or temperament. So, people often recognize or become aware of a preference for one given conflict approach only when they encounter some behavior that feels foreign or opposing to their own approach. For example, an avoider preparing to buy a car from a slick, competitive salesperson might have trouble communicating with someone who uses different words, expressions, and gestures to achieve different goals.

When others have opposing goals and rely on different negotiation tactics, they may be suspicious or feel uncomfortable or nervous about interacting with someone who uses different languages. Undoubtedly, we risk some communication failure and discomfort as we expand our normal communication habits, but we also put ourselves in a position for new, potentially helpful patterns and conflict outcomes.

While adults may lack the same mental flexibility characteristic of youth, we do not lose our ability to learn. Scientists now understand that humans are flexibly wired with the capacity to learn throughout a lifetime. In fact, as adults, we often enjoy several advantages over learning in childhood, including wider perspectives, a longer attention span, greater patience, and higher motivation to learn despite our more fixed wiring.

Several years ago, I tutored my friend Jill, who was trying to learn French for the first time as an adult. I sensed her eagerness to learn, along with an incentive to prepare for a future trip to Europe. At first, there were many moments of frustration when she could not easily recall what we had discussed before. But, as we sat together each week to review her French studies, I grew to admire her ability to not only learn, but to enjoy her emerging language skills. Jill formed a living example of an adult working to expand a somewhat fixed skill set to fulfill a certain dream of hers.

Workbook Questions:

- How have I tried to change my approaches to conflict as an adult?
- What has motivated me to change my conflict approaches throughout my life?
- What motivates me to consider my approaches to conflict now?

Do We Treat Other's Conflicts Differently Than Our Own?

As you learn about your native conflict approaches, consider whether you behave differently with your own personal conflicts than when you help others to manage theirs. It's natural to use different approaches with other people's conflicts because we think and feel differently about conflicts that do not pull on our emotions. Awareness of this tendency to manage personal and unrelated conflicts differently helps you not only to empathize with others, but also to more effectively think through what works and what does not work in conflict situations.

When recently called upon to manage a group conflict among volunteers at a community organization, I realized that I am more likely to ask good questions and reason through individuals' motivations when I am not involved in conflict. When helping others, I seek more to listen and evaluate evidence rather than react emotionally to the conflict interaction like I did with my supervisor in the experience I related in chapter 1. When acting in a more professional role as a mediator, when I have no personal stake in the conflict, I tend to use more collaborative thinking and act on behalf of all involved parties.

In addition, with others' conflicts, I can set aside emotion to focus on technique and strategy. My feelings are not usually escalated, so I can see the big picture to work out effective resolutions. To be effective, I need to be able to empathize with the people I help through conflict, but my thinking brain usually leads the way rather than my emotions.

On the flip side, if I'm the person in conflict—whether with a peer, a child, a spouse, or even a stranger—I tend to focus on my own emotions and feelings of justification. When emotions come into play, it's harder for me to think through options that will satisfy everyone's interests. Honestly, I tend to focus on my own interests unless I can calm my emotions. While I'm working on curbing these patterns, they feel more instinctual. Still, given some practice with different conflict approaches, I am learning to be more flexible.

Likewise, when I'm helping a close girlfriend through conflict, I may exercise a lot of patience, show empathy, listen carefully, and try to see things from my friend's perspective. But with my children, I am not always as patient or under-standing. Instead of listening to them carefully, I may ask them to go to their room if they need to cry or vent. Both my adult friend and my child may be dealing with similar feelings of insecurity in a relationship, but I tend to help them manage their personal conflicts in somewhat different ways with both positive and negative results. I share this because some of us tend to treat our children's conflicts more lightly than our friends' or other adults' conflicts as if our children's feelings are less important than our friend's feelings.

As we become aware of the tendency to manage certain conflicts differently, we might ask ourselves how effective these different approaches are in each context. Are we giving equal value to the thoughts, feelings, and experiences of our children, just as we would help our friends through their conflicts?

Workbook Questions:

- Do I take the same steps with my personal conflicts as I would with someone else's?

- If there are differences between how I handle my conflict and how I counsel or assist someone else through their conflicts, how do my approaches differ? Why do I think they differ?

- How does my handling of my children's conflicts differ with how I approach conflicts between my peers at work? With friends? With other adults in my life?

- What approaches seem to work best with my peers?

- How can I transfer some of these more effective approaches into my home life?

Teaching Your Children Effective Conflict Management Skills

Since we know that people learn languages and certain other skills more easily when they are young, I am focusing on teaching my children about communication and conflict management so that these five conflict approaches will come more easily to them as they follow their own life journeys. This means I teach them by explaining, but, more importantly, through helping them apply skills in the context of their own daily conflicts. I expect this to be a long process, and we will all gradually learn how to effectively manage conflict in different situations.

By helping my children become aware of conflict approaches and making progress by practicing, my children and I have a better chance of enjoying successful relationships, meeting our needs, and being able to help others in all different life situations. Like foreign language fluency, conflict fluency provides a way to communicate and build connections with other people who at first appear and behave differently from us, but who are part of the same human family.

By equipping our children in this way, we teach them more than words, but in a broader sense, how to interact with the world around themselves. Given the complexity of human interaction, we can provide constructive tools, skills, and perspectives to allow children to interact comfortably with people who think and behave differently than they do. In short, we have the chance to prepare children for all their relationships to come, fostering constructive communication patterns during the great flexibility of childhood.

For example, if I want my children to understand that their thoughts and feelings count in our family, I need to fill their lives with examples of and opportunities to practice compromising, accommodating, and collaborating in our home. If I'd like them to think for themselves and solve problems with others, I cannot expect always to compete or force my children to follow my rules. I need to use a blend of the five approaches to help give my children secure boundaries while emphasizing their capacity to act for themselves in constructive ways using all five general conflict approaches.

Workbook Questions:

- What kind of approaches do I use to resolve conflicts at home?

- Does my framework for conflict change in different contexts? If so, when and how does it differ?

- How can I incorporate more collaborative elements in my approach to conflict at home?

As parents, we have the challenge not only to understand our own conflict approaches, but also to teach our children how to appropriately apply these approaches in context. Fortunately, we have many opportunities in family life, especially with young children, to teach these approaches in theory and apply them in practice in our daily lives.

In the following section, I share one afternoon in my life

managing a variety of conflicts from all different approaches, depending upon the situation. As you read through my experiences, allow yourself to recall conflicts in your own home—those that ended well, and those that you wish had ended differently. This section prepares us to see how critical our role as our children's teachers is and how quickly we may need to switch conflict approaches depending upon the person and circumstance.

Examples of the Five Conflict Approaches in Context

One Afternoon in the Taylor Household

During one eight-hour period, I used a variety of conflict approaches to manage my own and my children's conflict situations. I approached each situation differently depending on my goals and the circumstances related to my children's goals, skills, and experience. As you read through the overview of the five conflict approaches with examples from my experiences, consider how you can flexibly adapt your conflict management approaches to deal with the various conflict situations you encounter on any given day.

12:00 p.m. **Avoiding and Accommodating** with a Craigslist responder

3:55 p.m. **Coaching toward Compromise** with my youngest son and second son

3:57 p.m. **Coaching toward Collaborating** with my oldest son and neighbor boys

4:00 p.m. **Coaching toward Collaborating** with my second son, my youngest daughter, and neighbor

4:15 p.m. **Collaborating** with my oldest daughter

4:30 p.m. **Competing** with two of my sons

5:45 p.m. **Competing and Compromising** with my youngest daughter

6:15 p.m. **Competing** with my oldest son

7:30 p.m. **Coaching toward Compromise** with my oldest son

Example of Avoiding and Accommodating: Armageddon and the Craigslist's Responder

One morning, Dan, a retired man wearing a ratty t-shirt and jeans, showed up at my door to retrieve the free Bowflex machine I had posted on Craigslist. He mentioned that he was living with fifteen dogs in the foothills of the Rocky Mountains, and I believed him because I could hardly breathe while I was in his presence due to the intense dog smell. While his heavy dog smell repulsed my senses, I had no need to mention it: we would have only that one brief meeting as virtual strangers in the exchange of property then go our separate ways. I avoided bringing up a sensitive topic with a stranger whom I would interact with briefly.

Before he left, he asked for a minute of my time. He

then warned me about how Armageddon would begin that summer with UN troops forming battalions along the US-Mexico border. As he explained that another solar system was about to enter our galaxy, I fully realized that I was in an avoiding-accommodating scenario.

Whether Rick had taken too many drugs in his youth or suffered from mental illness, I realized that he was not operating on all cylinders. While I wanted to keep writing my book, I had just a few minutes to interact with Rick as he disassembled the Bowflex and shared his warning about Armageddon. I had little to lose by briefly accommodating him and giving up some of my limited time by listening to his story and nodding my head as he shared his warnings. I even thanked him for the warning, though I contributed little to the conversation.

Example of Teaching and Coaching Compromise: Splitting the Last Piece of Pie

As my kids returned home from school, I promised my youngest son, Ben, the last piece of Aunt Kate's apple pie for his after-school treat. He enthusiastically ran into the house from the bus stop before I realized that his nine-year-old brother, Jack, was going to want some of that pie too. As I entered the house with Jack in tow, we both saw Ben grinning with his one piece of pie ready to heat up in the microwave. He was happy, almost triumphant, that he had secured the last piece of the coveted pie.

I quickly realized my mistake in promising him the

pie before Jack had had a chance to claim some, so I had to backpedal a bit to get Ben to see the light: compromise was required with eating the last piece of pie. As I made the request ("Ben, will you split the pie with Jack?"), Ben stood defiant, pie in hand, claiming that it wasn't fair for him to split the pie because I had already promised him the whole piece. I apologized for promising him something that wasn't fair to Jack and asked that he split the pie. Ben wasn't standing for a renegotiation of terms.

In a change of strategy, I asked Ben, "What if Jack had the only piece of pie? Would you want him to split it with you?" Ben looked skeptical, but began to see the situation from Jack's perspective. I could tell that Ben needed only a little more coaching or motivation to agree to split the pie.

As my final offer, like an auctioneer, cheerleader, and coach at the same time, I suggested, "What if we split the pie and I add a little vanilla ice cream to each piece?" We usually only have ice cream on Fridays to limit our sugar intake, but I decided to throw in a compromise myself since I had created the conflict in the first place by promising something unfair to one of my children. The boys enthusiastically accepted the offer and enjoyed eating their "prize" treats out on the deck in the sun. Fortunately, my other three children had not been interested in the pie!

Example of Coaching Toward Collaborating: Keeping Things Cool During Basketball

Just before Ethan headed out the door to play basketball with two competitive seven-year-olds (my youngest son, Ben, and our neighbor, Matt), I took Ethan aside to coach him a bit about helping the younger boys collaborate with each other. I asked him to use his skills to try to make it fair so these two super competitive boys who sometimes disagreed about fouls and rules didn't wind up hating each other and having a bad time. I didn't give Ethan a specific method (he was almost eleven at the time), but asked him to be aware of the potential for conflict in the basketball game.

As I stepped outside five to ten minutes later to check on the boys, I was happy to see Ethan playing the "lay-up man" who helped each boy when it was their turn on offense. Ethan balanced out the skills of the game to keep it even, but also regulated with some refereeing on the side. The boys seemed happy and engaged in playing.

Example of Coaching Toward Collaborating: Three's a Crowd Playdate

At least once a week, our neighbor, Olivia, comes over to play with my middle-son, Jack. Amy also likes to invite Olivia over to play. One day, after Olivia accepted an invitation from Amy, Jack came into the kitchen feeling so sad that Olivia was playing with Amy.

Right away, I found the girls outside and instructed them to make sure that they played with Jack while Olivia was over. We spent a minute or two talking over what that might look like during the playdate. The girls readily agreed to include Jack fully once we talked about Jack's thoughts and feelings and ways to make sure everyone played well together.

As the saying goes, "three's a crowd." We joke about it, but a friendship or even a playdate of three can be challenging and conflict-ridden. Parents can anticipate these conflicts and plan for teaching (and enforcing) collaborative efforts among our children. We may also emphasize taking turns to avoid threesomes, if necessary. Even adults often need help with managing unbalanced social groups.

Example of Collaborating: Modifying Emma's Practice Schedule for Playing Violin

I didn't want to engage in collaborating with Emma about practicing the violin, but as she nears twelve years old and has gotten involved with many other activities, I have had to ease back on how often they practice their musical instruments. In the past, I had mirrored some of Amy Chua's more coercive "Tiger Mom" tactics, demanding instrument practice every day, but I noticed that my daughter needed something different in managing this conflict between us.

Emma had been taking violin lessons for about four years with fairly good results, but she had not been willing to practice much for the past year or so. In fact, I found myself regularly nagging her to practice a mere fifteen to twenty minutes a day to maintain her current ability. Frustrated by our constant battle of wills, I finally approached her about the subject with a collaborative mindset.

She and I had a lengthy discussion about her practicing over the following couple of weeks. We compromised and changed her practice schedule to three days out of five instead of all five like I had wanted. Most importantly, Emma revealed her frustrations about not progressing in violin like she wanted to. As we discussed possibilities for future playing, including continuing private lessons and playing in the middle school orchestra, we decided together that she would keep playing through the summer, begin orchestra in school the next year, and quit private lessons while she plays at school.

Through honest discussion, we found a way to preserve Emma's interest in violin, but in a way that met Emma's social and musical motivations and my desire for her to continue playing. We had to spend time to find the right balance between our different interests, but we created a plan for how to move forward the next year without revisiting the same conflict about practicing each day. On a side note, not only did Emma enjoy orchestra, but she soon asked me to hire a private violin teacher again so that she could learn more on her own.

Example of Competing: Earning Money to Buy Pokémon Cards

Ethan and Ben wanted to earn money to buy more Pokémon cards. I suggested to Ethan that he could spread mulch to earn six dollars per hour. Ben also wanted to earn money by spreading the mulch. Ethan grew furious because he thought if Ben joined in, he would only be making $3 per hour. In short, Ethan thought Ben would be "stealing" his opportunity to make money. I explained that they could both work on the job and that I would pay each of them by the hour for the work they performed. In short, they would not have to split the hourly wage.

While Ethan wanted exclusive rights to spread the mulch, as the hiring manager, I could set the terms with both Ethan and Ben and compete with their different expressed views. I took the opportunity to explain that they could work together and both earn the same hourly wage even if they worked together on the same project. In addition, I suggested other projects so that they could continue to work as long as they liked. Ultimately, I had the chance to explain common practices from the working world of adults where people usually work on teams, but get paid individually for the work they contribute to a project. In a way, you are competing with fellow employees, but you're still working for the same boss for individual pay. In a competitive conflict sense, a boss may set and enforce certain terms that must be followed for payment.

Example of Competing and Compromising: Running out of Lunch Money Due to Poor Management

Our house rule has always been that each child may buy one extra snack in the cafeteria each week. Knowing this, I added just enough money to each child's account to get through the end of the year. Very early in the spring, Amy ran out of lunch money because she had bought too many extra snacks from the cafeteria during the year. I was upset that she hadn't been following our rules for the cafeteria.

The boys overheard my conversation with Amy about overspending, so they got involved in blaming and accusing her of breaking our house rules. Amy felt ashamed and ran crying to her room. Once she had calmed down, we discussed what to do: Should Amy have to take home lunches until the end of the year? Should I give her more lunch money, but make sure she promised not to not get any more snacks? We had set the rule, but had not anticipated its violation and did not have a plan for noncompliance, which often creates significant conflict.

Because she is young, I decided to give Amy more lunch money with the express promise (and a note to the cafeteria staff to help enforce the decision) not to buy any more extra snacks or treats in addition to her regular lunch. She lost the snack privilege, but not her regular lunch. That was our compromise with each other because I did have to spend more money than I had intended, and Amy kept buying school lunches, while giving up some of her favorite snacks.

Example of Competing (with Some Collaborating): Upholding Family Rules

In our house, the rules about using the computer are strict. Each child may have twenty minutes on an approved computer program after completing his or her instrument practice—an idea which I had created, but everyone had accepted. While I stepped out briefly to drive my oldest daughter to an activity at the middle school, my three sons jumped on the computer to watch an episode of a Pokémon video—something they know to be strictly against the rules, especially because I was not home while they were on the Internet.

As I walked in the door from the garage, I noticed that everyone jumped back from the dinner table and quickly tried to put the computer away. I easily guessed what they had been doing and secured three quick confessions to the infraction. In a competitive stance to defend our long-standing home rules, I revoked computer privileges for the rest of the day and warned all three about breaking our house rules. I added a further warning about greater consequences if we experienced any more problems.

Feeling unnatural about competitively laying down the law so firmly, during dinnertime, I asked the boys about what they thought the rules for the computer should be. After some discussion, Ethan said, "I think we should keep the rules we have; they seem good." Surprisingly, the other boys agreed.

While I had second-guessed my strategy of staying firm with our rules, the boys had accepted them. I just needed to enforce what we had already decided as a family. In competing, we may simply be enforcing or following up on decisions we have already agreed to. In this case, I didn't need to compromise or collaborate further with my kids because we had already been through the rule-setting process. If breaking this rule comes up repeatedly in future, we might reconsider as a family how to approach computer time with a more collaborative approach.

Example of Teaching and Coaching Toward Compromise: Splitting the Fruit Leather

Later that evening, during a ride home from a school concert, Ethan found a lone wrapped fruit leather in the cubby near his usual seat in the car. He announced his find and started to unwrap it and was about to take a first bite. Knowing that everyone was hungry, tired, and craving the surprise find, I anticipated large pushback from his brothers and sisters.

Similar to the situation with Ben and the lone piece of pie, I asked Ethan, "How would you feel if Jack found the fruit leather and ate it all himself in front of you?" Ethan's brothers and sister also chimed in about this thought-provoking question, saying that they would be mad because it wasn't fair.

Ethan gave my question and his siblings' comments some consideration, then under some pressure (and, hopefully, with some foresight) decided to share the fruit leather equally among them. This was not his first inclination, but he was motivated by a thoughtful question that inspired him to see the situation from a different perspective. He chose to compromise. I tried not to force Ethan to do it, but coached him to develop an alternative view on his treasure find.

Conclusion

In each of these real-life conflict scenarios, I chose different conflict approaches to meet my needs and goals, as well as the needs and goals of the children and the circumstances. While the outcomes weren't perfect, as a family, we are setting a precedent for principled flexibility and a commitment to leaning how to manage conflict. We have a more significant conflict management tool belt to draw from that allows for more positive results.

You will encounter different conflict situations in your own home, but with the five approaches, you will have a larger range of options for handling them. As you gain more awareness, you will be more conscious about the tools you choose to use and how you use them with your most important students: your children. While your children may not always appear to be listening, they are watching and aware of how you choose to handle both their conflicts and your own.

Having gained an initial awareness of your own conflict patterns and behaviors, you can now turn to understanding your children's patterns and potential for learning constructive conflict management. First, I review socio-emotional and intellectual development highlights for preschoolers through twelve-year-olds. Following the child development chapter, I focus on the significance of the sibling relationship, sibling conflict, and typical patterns of parent response to sibling conflict. In the mediation chapters, I blend an understanding of our own conflict approaches and attitudes with those of our children.

Chapter 3 Summary

Learning Conflict Approaches as Children

- Children first learn conflict management through observation, imitation, and direct training. Some of our habits are more constructive than others.

- Children imitate the behavior of their role models, even before they fully understand conflict and have a vocabulary for talking about conflict.

Learning New Languages and Approaches as Adults

- Despite more limited brain flexibility, adults have the advantage of patience, perspective, and experience.

Preparing to Teach Your Children New Languages

- It's important to be aware of the tendency to treat children's conflicts differently than you would your own or your peers' conflicts.

Teaching and Using the Five Conflict Languages in Context

- Reviewing real life experiences helps us to apply the best approach when conflicts arise.

CHAPTER 4

OVERVIEW OF CHILD DEVELOPMENT MILESTONES

Twelve years ago, as I held ten-month-old Emma in my arms, she suddenly said the word "cat" out loud. Emma's first word! We didn't even have a cat, but my husband and I were ecstatic that she said something intelligible at such a young age. From that point on, we made very deliberate efforts to teach her new words, like "mama" and "dada."

Of course, we didn't try to teach her anything incorrect about the English language or criticize her for saying things wrong; we trusted that, in time, she would grow into more full expression and the ability to communicate more effectively. We expected her to continue growing in her ability to express herself and use the English language to communicate effectively with those around her. In short, we understood that while Emma's language skills were immature and still developing, we could encourage and help her along the way.

Contrast of Parent Approaches to Early Conflict Resolution Development

Parents are in a similar position to teach communication skills and conflict resolution that, like the development of language, require deliberate effort, patience, and understanding of children's developmental capacity. Just as Emma didn't learn English all at once, but benefitted considerably from our time and attention to encourage, correct, and directly teach her over many years, our children may not learn conflict resolution skills in one sitting. In fact, learning how to resolve conflict represents a series of major stepping stones in a child's social development.

Parents don't usually treat conflict resolution skills the same as early language acquisition. In the quest for peace or quick reconciliation, they ignore the long-term view on conflict skills development. In frustration, fatigue, and the stress associated with conflict situations, parents fail to offer the same type of gentle correction of mistakes or to demonstrate tolerance for children's inability to manage conflict and the emotional frustration that results.

Scolding, Punishing, or Ignoring

Imagine that your four-year-old son is screaming and crying because his older brother just grabbed his favorite new toy and has begun playing with it in the other room. As parents of preschoolers, you may expect such outbursts and lack of skills, but what happens when your ten-year-old screams in in a similar way when her brother teases her about her new braces, for example?

In both situations, we can demand that children stop screaming and apologize to each other. But often we scold or shame kids when they make mistakes in managing conflict *without teaching them more effective ways to handle their opposing goals and the anger they feel.* Sometimes, we even demonstrate our own lack of social skills (and patience) by screaming or yelling back that our kids just need to obey and be quiet. In other words, we expect children to apply skills to manage their emotions and conflicts that we still struggle with.

Screaming, crying, whining, and everything related to those behaviors irritates most people, especially parents of young children who deal with a lot more of it. But consider the language acquisition example again. In her beginning years of English mastery, if I had constantly scolded my toddler for making mistakes, she might have stopped trying to talk. I understood her developmental capacity with language learning and, therefore, didn't chastise her for her lack of skills.

In a more extreme example, what if I had assumed Emma could learn English correctly without anyone teaching her? For any attentive parent, the thought sounds ridiculous! Still, I remember a coworker who traveled extensively for her job bemoaning the fact that her young daughter spoke Spanish as her first language because the Spanish-speaking nanny was raising her child. There is nothing wrong with learning Spanish as a first language, but the mother didn't speak Spanish, so she and her daughter could not communicate effectively. What is not deliberately taught about communicating may be subject to the whims of circumstance, peers, school setting, or other influential adults.

In the alternative, parents might ignore children's conflicts, put on their headphones, and tell the children to work it out themselves. Parents often do ignore their children's fighting, despite knowing, but not realizing, that children often lack the fundamental skills to negotiate and collaboratively problem solve. We might even assume that kids are willfully fighting to get attention or to make themselves miserable. Do children really want to be miserable themselves or to make us miserable? I believe that both children and adults rarely seek to intentionally make themselves miserable, but often lack the skills, motivation, or understanding to meet their needs effectively. Perhaps, we need a new understanding about why are kids are fighting and what we can do about it.

Common Parent Biases About Our Children's Fighting

Given the constancy of some sibling conflict, you might incorrectly assume that children enjoy fighting or that they are only seeking attention. Perhaps, you assume that children have the necessary communication skills, but lack the proper motivation or "good" character to resolve conflicts effectively. Certainly, parents have inaccurately suggested that children lack the right character traits to communicate and resolve conflicts effectively, as if there is nothing a parent or child can do to change damaging social patterns and behavior.

The Fundamental Attribution Error

Parents tend to attribute certain behavior to character traits rather than to environmental factors described by the fundamental attribution error. According to this theory, people tend to attribute negative qualities to someone else's character, as opposed to understanding how environmental factors like heat, fatigue, hunger, and stress affect another person's behavior and may not reflect their overall character. In contrast, we tend to avoid negatively attributing our own bad behavior to our character, but instead include a relief clause for ourselves based on circumstance.

Parents may blame children for fighting with each other, as if children want to fight and possess particularly negative personalities or character flaws. Instead of evaluating children's character, parents benefit from focusing on environmental factors, such as lack of skill and the particular problem that needs to be solved. When trying to explain why children's behavior can be so challenging, well-known child psychologist Dr. Ross Greene explains that children will behave well and make good decisions if they can. Greene claims that children will choose constructive paths, if they have the skills to do so and know how to resolve certain types of problems.

Rather than blame children for "flawed" characters or ourselves for our "flawed" parenting, the best course is to focus on helping children (and ourselves) gain more sophisticated conflict resolution skills and examine the unresolved problems we face in our personal and family lives. In short, by becoming aware of our own skills, our children's skills, and by identifying the real issues we encounter in our homes, we can begin to make needed changes.

As parents, we can become aware of our habits in conflict situations, our habitual conflict styles that we've developed throughout our lives and that match our native temperaments and personalities. We can also understand the pros and cons of our approaches to different types of conflict. However, parenting demands that we assess and manage children's conflicts with each other, and not just with us. This conflict management focused on others leads us to assess our conflict resolution skills along with our children's. This assessment of our children and ourselves propels us toward becoming a guide and support rather than a judge of our children's abilities in resolving conflicts.

Assessing Our Own Social Skills Alongside Our Children's Skills

Throughout a lifetime of learning and social interaction, people acquire many different social skills. To communicate our ideas effectively to other people and to negotiate differences in human interaction, adults might develop many different communication skills, including this list drawn from a communications website simply titled: Communication Skills.

- Taking responsibility for what we communicate
- Claiming ownership for what we communicate

- Preparing to listen
- Encouraging a speaker to speak more
- Reflecting on what others say
- Adjusting our thought process to consider differences of opinion
- Being open minded
- Acknowledging differences in values, beliefs, and actions
- Assessing others' messages without being judgmental
- Accepting feedback
- Being assertive
- Sharing our thoughts
- Sharing our feelings
- Conveying what we want to say to others without commanding or dictating terms
- Being aware of the information we are receiving
- Calmly repeating to emphasize your message
- Addressing people by name
- Explaining a concept differently so that all present understand it at their level
- Resolving conflicts so that the outcome is a win-win for all
- Being concise and clear
- Conveying thoughts in a focused and concrete manner
- Expressing empathy

- Explaining objectively without evaluating
- Providing specific details to support our claims
- Monitoring emotional reactions and filtering out irrational thoughts
- Projecting oneself into the audience's point of view

This is an exceptionally long list of communication skills, but instead of becoming overwhelmed by the depth and breadth of the list, consider which skills are most helpful to you personally and which skills you want your children to learn first.

Workbook Questions:

- Which communication skills from the list do I have now?
- Which communication skills would I like to develop?
- Which communication skills do I want my children to develop?

As with language acquisition, you could overwhelm your children (and yourself) with such long, detailed lists of sophisticated communication skills. Instead, pare down the bigger list to a shorter one appropriate to your growing children's conflict resolution needs and development:

- Sharing personal feelings and perspectives without blaming or accusing
- Listening to other people's feelings and perspectives

without interrupting

- Asking clarifying questions
- Brainstorming potential solutions to a problem without criticizing other people's suggestions
- Discussing the pros and cons of different ideas
- Selecting a solution that meets our needs as well as the other parties' needs

With these six basic communication skills in hand, adults and children are more likely to succeed in resolving conflict with collaborative approaches, like mediation. In that light, consider a few questions about you and your children's current communication skills.

Workbook Questions:

- Which of the six basic conflict management skills do I model successfully with my significant other and my children now?
- Which communication skills are my children working on right now?
- Which of these specific conflict resolution skills would I like my children to develop?
- What is the most pressing need for conflict resolution that we have in our family right now? (Perhaps, the conflict we are dealing with right now represents the most pressing need.)

Scaffolding Children's Conflict Resolution Skills Development

Just as parents assist children with language acquisition, we help our children by scaffolding or assisting their growth when needed. As children master certain skills, we can pull away gradually and allow them to exercise autonomy. In 2015, I recorded an experience about helping my youngest daughter, Amy (aged four at the time), gain enough confidence to ride a bike on her own around our hilly neighborhood. I ran alongside Amy as she pedaled her own bike, and only directly assisted her when she needed it. Here is an excerpt from my recorded tale:

"I ran alongside Amy as she rode her bike. It has been best for her to learn balance on her own—training wheels don't teach that. Balance is a skill that must be acquired through one's own efforts either by a small bike adapted to the size of the child or much later with greater difficulty and risk when they're higher off the ground.

As Amy rode around our neighborhood, I put my hand on her shoulder only while she rode downhill to reassure her. I pushed her uphill because she only has one gear, which represents skills (developmental constraints, perhaps)."

Just as Amy learned how to ride a bike quickly given many early learning opportunities, a bike her size, and my running beside her, kids can succeed in developing conflict resolution skills as we learn to scaffold or support them. As they gain confidence and increased autonomy, we then slowly pull away.

Early Childhood Development Learning Potential

At four years old, Amy learned to ride a bike rapidly given the proper tools, support, and coaching per her development. Likewise, during the first four to five years of life, children learn socio-emotional skills at an incredibly fast pace and set many patterns that influence development outcomes throughout their lifetimes.

During early childhood, children put the building blocks in place that will serve as the foundation for all later development and intellectual growth. Children learn most quickly through direct explanations and parental modeling of positive behavior. Most of children's first lessons take place in the home, which is the most important socializing force in their lives. As parents, we can greatly facilitate our children's growth and development, while maintaining a perspective about natural developmental milestones common to all children.

Child Development Basics for Preschoolers and School-Aged Children

To understand our children's ability to collaborate and participate in parent-led mediation, we will briefly explore fundamentals of early childhood development focused on communication and problem solving. While not exhaustive, this information can help parents remain patient as they teach and model positive communication skills and principles for children. When parents understand their children's abilities with average child development milestones, they are in a better position to guide children toward constructive conflict resolution habits.

For specific research materials used throughout this chapter, please refer to the resources section for chapter 4 and blog postings on www.raisingmediators.com.

Preschoolers (Ages Three to Five)

Much of a child's basic brain infrastructure and neural wiring is in place by age four. Given the interplay of biology and environment, parents have a critical opportunity during these early years to set constructive patterns for social behavior through a child's most important relationships. Primarily, these key relationships take place in our homes alongside parents and siblings.

Autonomy

Preschooler behavior is characterized by two competing desires: to act independently of parents, but also to retreat into the love and security of a parent or another caregiver. Even from preschool years, children desire personal control and a sense of autonomy appropriate to their emerging physical and social skills.

Preschoolers still struggle with the idea of cause-and-effect relationships. They must learn this concept before they can separate right from wrong or unintentional versus intended harm. During the preschool years, they will gain a better grasp of causal relationships and the intentions behind their own behavior and that of others.

Language Development

Preschoolers rapidly expand their verbal understanding from about three hundred to five hundred words at three years old to nearly four thousand words, and they use about two thousand words of those words regularly toward the end of the preschool years. This rapid verbal expansion allows pre-schoolers to interact with others in a much more sophisticated way than previously possible. As a consequence, preschoolers can negotiate about conflicts more effectively with their siblings, although they still lag behind their older siblings in several different areas of development.

Self-Control and Emotional Regulation

Early childhood development specialists consider four areas of self-control and emotional regulation that preschoolers need to master on their path to social development. These four areas quoted in child development researcher Dr. Sandra V. Sandy's work include the following:

- **Movement**—Before age six or seven, children have a hard time stopping an action already in progress (e.g., turning off a video game or TV)

- **Emotions**—Before age four, children have little control over the intensity of their emotions (e.g., tantrums over large and small matters)

- **Reflection**—Before age six, children commonly fail to reflect on how well they have performed (e.g., does your child visualize a great piano performance before a recital?)

- **Gratification**—Children younger than twelve find it difficult to refuse immediate gratification or wait for a better choice later (e.g., the famous marshmallow test to determine if kids could wait fifteen minutes without eating one marshmallow to earn a second one)

Positive Social Development

Preschoolers generally focus on themselves and tend to understand conflict in terms of "what I can't do because of how other people are behaving." In the past, child development theorists critically underestimated preschool aged children's capacity to empathize with others and understand the perspective of another person. Social scientists now observe that children as young as two years old show concern for others in distress, which illustrates a first step of thinking beyond one's own feelings and interests relating to others.

Perspective Taking

Typical preschoolers have difficulty separating their point of view from that of others. They generally lack the ability to distinguish between their own perceptions of an event and that of another child or adult. They tend to have difficulty accepting the idea that there are multiple possible explanations for a conflict that does not have a clear wrongdoer.

In addition, preschoolers do not understand cause-and-effect relationships or how one thing affects another, so they often have a hard time explaining how others are thinking and behaving. For example, when they are punished, preschoolers tend to feel *that* they did something wrong because they have been punished, but they may not understand *what* they did wrong. They are unsure about causal relationships and look to authority figures, such as parents or teachers, to explain the cause behind certain outcomes.

Older research studies demonstrate that children younger than eight years old have difficulty seeing the perspective of another person, but new evidence suggests that even preschoolers can learn to imitate basic perspective taking and emotional understanding skills by learning to reflect what their parents or other close caregivers say.

Empathy

Despite preschoolers' natural difficulty to understand multiple explanations and perspectives on a conflict situation, they usually can tell the difference between real and pretend feelings, but cannot explain their evaluations. In the past, child development theorists believed that preschoolers lacked the capacity to demonstrate much empathy, but recent research suggests that preschoolers have much greater empathetic potential than previously thought.

In preschoolers, empathy first develops as parents help them explore their own emotions. Following a more egocentric approach, parents can help guide children to understanding how others feel through direct teaching and modeling of caring and compassionate communication with others.

Peer Influence

During the preschool years, children engage in all types of play with peers, but remain highly connected to their care-givers. They spend a lot of time with their parents, which changes as they move into their elementary, middle, and high school years.

Dr. Sandy recommends several steps parents can take to help their children develop conflict resolution skills during children's critical learning years. These parent steps include:

- Helping preschoolers talk about their emotions (emotional understanding)
- Helping preschoolers understand their own emotions and that of others (perspective taking)
- Modeling and using verbal reinforcement of acts of kindness and understanding
- Avoiding shaming children (this promotes a child's avoidance of adults rather than the child's learning)
- Promoting peer relationships that encourage pre-schoolers to develop empathy and moral develop-ment (a sense of right and wrong)
- Practicing an authoritarian parenting style, which is characterized by a firm sense of rules and parent control, but also by a warm parent-child relationship involving discussion and parent-child negotiation

Given the tremendous cognitive, social, emotional, and physical growth preschoolers undergo, parents can help them by teaching positive social behaviors from their earliest days. Even before they understand the meaning behind certain behaviors, children may learn to imitate parents' and caregivers' positive communication and problem-solving skills. An early start with positive patterns provides a solid foundation of learning for a lifetime.

Workbook Questions for Parents of Preschoolers

- What have I noticed about my child's autonomy needs?
- How would I describe my child's language development?
- What have I noticed about my child's ability to control his or her emotions?
- How would I describe my child's prosocial development, in terms of empathy and perspective taking?
- How does my child interact with his or her peers? What kind of influence do my child's peers have in his or her life?
- After answering these questions, how do I see my child's individual skills gaps or strengths?

School-Aged Children (Ages Six to Twelve)

From ages six to twelve, children spend an increasing amount of time away from parents and more time with peers, so their social world usually expands significantly. Given children's increasing maturity, cognitive abilities, verbal expression, and strengthened ability to self-regulate, six- to twelve-year-olds naturally desire to act independently of their parents. At this age, children adopt attitudes of give-and-take and compatibility. Many children focus on gaining social acceptance from their peers, and positive self-esteem is an important related goal.

Autonomy
In spite of their growing independence from parents through attending school and other organized activities, children this age still rely heavily on authority figures, like parents and teachers, to establish the norms, rules, and values of everyday social interaction.

Language Development
During this stage, children gain significant verbal ability and expression. Even with this increased language ability, children in middle childhood still lack the ability to think in terms of the abstract and prefer more tangible, concrete references and examples.

Self-Control and Emotional Regulation
Despite children's increased ability to self-regulate their behavior once they reach middle childhood, these abilities are not yet fully mature. Children are still motivated by self-centered goals, but they begin to reason beyond their own point of view when confronted with a conflict situation.

To encourage positive patterns of self-control, parents of six-to-twelve-year-olds will have the most success if they appeal to their children's sense of cooperation rather than obedience because of their growing autonomy needs and desires. In addition to appealing to children's sense of cooperation, parents should be aware that children this age tend to credit their failures to a lack of innate ability rather than a reflection of personal effort. As parents, it helps to be aware of this tendency when correcting children's poor behavior or performance to avoid unduly discouraging or shaming children.

Positive Social Development

Children in the middle-childhood years develop a sense of equity or justice in relationships. They may view events as an exchange system: a reward for a good act, or a punishment for a bad act. With a conflict situation, children tend to believe that one person is responsible for a given conflict and that any type of resolution should come from the "guilty" person.

Given this tendency toward unilateral blame and unilateral restitution, parents can encourage children to participate in conversations that help children explore alternative solutions and cause-and-effect thinking (i.e., what events led to these results?).

Perspective Taking

Children in this age group can make inferences about others' perspectives and feelings, but they typically have a hard time thinking about their own feelings and someone else's at the same time. Because of this difficulty, they usually stick to their own view of events or turn to an authority figure, like a parent, coach, or teacher, as a point of reference.

Empathy

Some children may still have a hard time distinguishing between their own interests and other people's goals and interests, although their abilities will likely have improved considerably since their preschool years.

Peer Influence

Peers play a very significant role in children's life during these ages. As children seek social acceptance from their peers and spend more time with them and away from their parents, children engage in all kinds of autonomous problem solving.

While children this age tend to have fewer conflicts with friends, boys and girls differ somewhat on what issues trigger conflict with their peers. Generally, boys disagree about power issues and attempt to seek dominance and what they want when in conflict with their male peers. Girls tend to focus their disagreements on interpersonal matters and seek to damage relationships or exclude as a means of resolving disagreements. So, boys and girls already demonstrate different conflict resolution patterns that influence how they behave as adolescents and adults.

Workbook Questions for Parents of School-Aged Children

- What have I noticed about my child's autonomy needs?
- How would I describe my child's language development?
- What have I noticed about my child's ability to self-regulate and control his or her emotions?
- How would I describe my child's prosocial development, in terms of empathy and perspective taking?
- How does my child interact with his or her peers? What kind of influence do my child's peers have in his or her life?
- After answering these questions, what do I think are my child's skills gaps or strengths?

Conclusion

By recognizing key child development milestones, parents are more likely to treat children's conflict management attempts with greater patience and perspective. While preschoolers can imitate constructive communication behaviors, parents still need to scaffold their conflict management behavior, especially with their more mature, sophisticated older siblings. School-aged children still lack abstract thinking and benefit from parents balancing the need to teach them while respecting their children's sense of autonomy.

Chapter 4 Summary

Assessing Our Communication Skills Alongside Our Children's Skills

- Understanding our own tendencies toward bias about our children's conflicts

- The fundamental attribution error: People tend to credit their faults to circumstance and others' faults or shortcomings to character.

Six Communication Skills Essential to Constructive Conflict Resolution

- Sharing personal feelings and perspectives without blaming or accusations

- Listening to other people's feelings and perspectives without interrupting

- Asking clarifying questions

- Brainstorming potential solutions to a problem without criticizing other people's suggestions

- Discussing the pros and cons of different ideas

- Selecting a solution that meets our needs as well as the other parties' needs

Scaffolding Children's Conflict Resolution Skills Development

Parents support their children's conflict-management efforts, but gradually pull away as they develop skills and gain experience.

Early Childhood Development Learning Potential

Preschoolers

- *Autonomy*: Preschoolers often have competing desires to be independent while still desiring the security of parents' love.

- *Language Development*: Preschoolers experience rapid changes that allow for greater interaction with others.

- *Self-control and Emotional Regulation*: Preschoolers struggle to understand cause-and-effect relationships. They have a hard time being disrupted during an activity. They usually have little control over the intensity of their emotions.

- *Prosocial Development*: Preschoolers focus mostly on themselves and understand conflict as what they can't do because of how others are behaving.

- *Perspective Taking*: Preschoolers have difficulty separating their own point of view from another person's, but can imitate perspective-taking skills if modeled well.

- *Empathy*: Preschoolers have difficulty in understanding other's perspectives, but are still able to model constructive empathetic behavior.

- *Peer Influence*: Preschoolers play with peers, but are more connected to caregivers. Often, they spend more time with adult caregivers than peers.

School-Aged Children

- *Autonomy*: School-aged children spend much more time away from parents and other caregivers. Usually, they desire more autonomy with peers and with making decisions. Despite their growing independence, they still look to authority figures to establish norms, rules, and values.

- *Language Development*: Children experience continued rapid verbal expansion, but lack the ability to think in abstract terms and respond best to tangible, concrete examples.

- *Self-control and Emotional Regulation*: Children are better able to manage disruption of activities. They are mostly motivated by self-centered goals, but begin to reason beyond their own point of view. Typically, they believe that poor performance is due to a lack of ability versus a lack of effort.

- *Prosocial Development*: Children focus on justice in relationships and usually believe only one person is responsible for a given conflict situation.

- *Perspective Taking*: Children can begin making inferences about others' perspectives and feelings, but usually have a hard time thinking about their own feelings and someone else's feelings at the same time.

- *Empathy*: Children may still have a hard time distinguishing between their own interests and other children's goals and interests.

- *Peer Influence*: Children spend much more time with peers who have greater influence in their lives. Children often seek social acceptance from peers and have many independent decision-making opportunities.

CHAPTER 5

THE SIBLING RELATIONSHIP AND SIBLING CONFLICT

At ten years old, Ethan is nearly five years older than his sister Amy, the youngest of our five children. Despite the difference in their ages, the presence of two brothers squeezed in between them, and being of different genders, Ethan and Amy share an intimate love-hate relationship with each other. Amy often screams as Ethan teases, pokes, and even sometimes tries to scare her on an average day. But, I've seen Amy deliberately try to annoy Ethan, who is nearly twice her size in height and weight. Despite her small size and position as the youngest child, I have heard Amy say provocative things to Ethan, including the too-oft-repeated statement that she "hates" Ethan. Amy usually interacts mostly with children her own age or younger, but still demonstrates self-confidence with older kids and adults, which reflects her unique experiences as the youngest of five children.

On other days, Amy snuggles in beside Ethan as he plays pretend games with her and even allows her to dictate some of the rules of the game. Though she is the youngest, Amy still exerts her will and seeks engagement with a much older and stronger sibling. On an average day, Ethan and Amy interact with each other frequently in both positive and negative ways, like most pairings of my children with each other. Of course, I try to curtail the negative patterns, but both Amy and Ethan are learning something about how to treat people who are different in age, gender, social and physical power, and physical, emotional, and social development.

Naturally, the way people relate to each other is impacted by their native temperaments, but also significantly by their key relationships, such as the sibling relationship. As Ethan and Amy's relationship shows, our children are working out who they are in the world in this fantastic experimental proving ground at home. Parents cannot change the temperaments of their children—parents have absolutely no control over that—but they can affect the environment children grow up in in very important ways.

In my life, I have seen Ethan listening attentively to younger kids in the neighborhood as he organizes casual football games at the park, playing by and enforcing the rules, and earning respect from younger children who really like him. Unlike many boys his age, Ethan pays attention to the younger kids he encounters and actually plays with them like he does with Amy at home. While it's difficult to separate the effects of nature and nurturing, I'm guessing that Ethan has learned how to treat younger children more fairly because of his relationship with Amy, and that Amy has learned to stick up for herself more because her brother has taken her thoughts, feelings, ideas, and well-being into account in daily interactions.

Each home is different, but I can see how my children are developing social skills right before my eyes as they interact with each other in both negative and positive ways. In the laboratory of the home, we can guide our children through their sibling relationships that will influence their social development and success in intimate relationships throughout their lives.

Siblings: Near-Peer Relationships

As mentioned earlier in the introduction section, almost 80 percent of children in Western society grow up with at least one sibling at home. As a result, many children experience their siblings as their first "near-peer" relationship, especially if the children are close in age. As near peers, siblings provide prime opportunities to discover the thoughts, feelings, and ambitions of other people. Our children learn about each other in both intimate positive and negative interactions.

As siblings, children learn how to interact with others who usually share fairly similar levels of personal power, life experience, developmental abilities, and, likely, personal experience with the same parents! Given such qualities, the nature of sibling relationships is often intimate and emotionally intense but stable over time. Through their sibling relationships, children learn and experience social situations that parents can't provide simply because we play different roles in their lives. The benefits that flow from social learning within sibling relationships hinges upon whether children enjoy constructive or destructive patterns of social interaction with each other.

Sibling Relationship Quality and Individual Social Development

During the past few decades, researchers have confirmed that our experiences with our siblings can influence our social development and interactions in significant ways into adolescence and adulthood, far beyond our early childhood experiences. Specifically, recent research links the quality of children's sibling relationships with their overall school adjustment, the quality of peer relationships, and the way children manage stress and negativity in their lives.

Internalizing vs. Externalizing Stress and Negativity

Based on the teachings of the late Dr. Marshall Rosenberg, an American psychologist who developed the nonviolent communication method, we each have four basic choices for dealing with negative messages or experiences in our relationships with others. In reaction to a negative message, we may

1. Blame ourselves
2. Blame others
3. Focus on understanding the thoughts of feelings of others
4. Seek to understand our own thoughts and feelings

These options are not unique to children, but represent choices that adults make too. Studies indicate that difficult sibling relationships directly influence children's (and the adults they become) tendencies to deal with stress in destructive ways, whether they internalize or externalize that stress.

Internalizing behavior describes habits when someone focuses stress and negativity inwardly and includes social withdrawal, feelings of loneliness or guilt, fearfulness, and not standing up for themselves. Typically, internalized stress and negativity remains hidden from others' view, but manifests in the behaviors mentioned.

Children who *externalize* stress and negativity tend to be more aggressive with the world outside of themselves. They might use physical aggression, destroy property, and try other dramatic gestures, such as running away from home. Studies show that girls and women struggle with internalizing stress more often, while boys and men externalize stress through acts of aggression or defiance.

Parents often discuss the perils of teenagers' internalizing or externalizing stress and negativity. But these harmful habits or behaviors originate much earlier in children's younger lives as they learn to interact and communicate with others. So, during the preschool and school-aged years, adults have a prime opportunity to influence children's development trajectory and the way they manage stress and negativity. As parents, we are in a central position to guide children's positive social behaviors by helping them develop healthy relationships with their siblings.

Prosocial Behavior Development Possibilities through Sibling Relationships

Prosocial behaviors are defined as voluntary behaviors that benefit others, such as being helpful, friendly, willing to share, and cooperative. For example, when there is only one empty swing on the playground, a child with prosocial behavior might offer to take turns on the swing rather than grab the swing quickly for herself. In the classroom, when another child drops a pencil or has trouble understanding an assignment, a prosocial child would offer to help when she sees the need arise. Prosocial behaviors help build connection between individuals in a variety of social settings.

Prosocial or socially constructive, helping behaviors are learned most effectively in early childhood through sibling relationships. In children's later years, they can learn new social behaviors and skills through greater effort. But, most prosocial behaviors are easier to teach to young children rather than retraining older children once they have developed negative social behaviors. According to Dr. Laurie F. Kramer, professor emerita of applied family studies at the University of Illinois, the essential positive social behaviors parents want to encourage in children include the following:

- **Positive Engagement** (Children play, enjoy, have fun, share mutual interests, and engage in conversation with siblings).

- **Cohesion** (Siblings learn to recognize and value experiences of help, support, cooperation, loyalty, and trust with each other).

- **Shared Experiences that Build Support** (Children learn to appreciate their siblings' unique knowledge of each other and of their family to strengthen bonds. They try to avoid using their intimate knowledge of each other to disadvantage their siblings).

- **Social and Emotional Understanding; Perspective Taking** (Children should acquire the ability to understand and respect their siblings' unique views, needs, goals, and interests in addition to their own).

- **Emotion Regulation** (Children are able to identify and manage their emotions and behaviors in emotionally challenging and frustrating situations with siblings).

- **Behavioral Control** (Children stop behaving in ways that siblings find undesirable, such as being bossy, teasing, embarrassing siblings in front of friends, tagging along, failing to respect personal boundaries and space, and using overly wild behaviors).

- **Forming Neutral or Positive Attributions** (In unclear conflict situations, children may form negative ideas about what has motivated their siblings' behaviors; children must learn to check or correct their faulty assumptions. Family members can help clarify children's intentions and share how others' behaviors affects them).

- **Problem Solving and Conflict Management** (Children need to be openly taught constructive conflict resolution methods to resolve conflicts with siblings).

Workbook Questions

- What mentioned prosocial communication skills are my children learning right now?
- How am I trying to teach my children any of these specific skills?
- What am I trying to work on in terms of my own personal communication skills?
- What is one essential prosocial behavior I can work on this week to help me and my children communicate more constructively?

Overview of Sibling Conflict

While parents may wish that sibling conflict would disappear, in moderate doses sibling conflict provides critical social learning opportunities for children. As we learn to resolve conflict, rather than run away from it, children (and parents) have more to gain than lose from moments of difference with each other. Conflict provides traction to propel us toward our ultimate parenting goal to raise self-reliant and compassionate children with the confidence and skill to resolve interpersonal problems in constructive ways.

Sibling Conflict Frequency

Siblings often fight with each other, especially if they are the same sex and close in age. In studies of preschool children, siblings develop conflicts with each other nearly eight times per hour. In other studies, three- to nine-year-old siblings fight at about the same rate as preschoolers. The number of conflicts siblings encounter goes down with increased maturity and verbal expression, but research suggests that significant sibling conflict continues into adolescence.

Workbook Questions:

- How often do my children fight with each other?
- Which of my children fight the most with each other?
- What do my children usually fight about?

Main Topics of Sibling Conflict

Children have unique personalities and characteristics, but researchers find that they fight about many of the same issues. Research confirms that most sibling conflict centers on property rights and privileges. Conflicts between siblings often arise in the following areas:

- Rights Violations (someone broke family/house rules)
- Fairness (equal distribution of desired items, even parent time and attention)
- Physical Aggression (hitting, scratching, kicking)
- Verbal Aggression (teasing, mocking, name-calling)
- Distraction from Tasks (one child tries to distract the other from activities)

Workbook Questions:

- How do my children usually fight with each other?

- How severe are my children's conflicts with each other?

Sibling Conflict Tactics

To understand sibling conflict issues and paths toward resolution, researchers have started to investigate how siblings resolve conflicts with each other and what types of parent intervention or nonintervention makes a difference to the outcome.

Just like adults, children resolve conflicts differently when an authority figure is present to oversee their tactics and process. To understand our role in helping children resolve conflict, it helps to know how children resolve conflicts without parent intervention or help.

Sibling Conflict Resolution Patterns without Parent Assistance

With or without parent intervention, sibling conflicts typically end in one of the four following ways:

- *Submission*: A child gives up his or her position.

- *No Resolution*: The conflict ends without resolving the issue.

- *Issue Compromise*: The children arrive at a middle position or a new solution in which both children gain something.

- *Relationship Compromise*: The children decide to take each other's feelings into account when dealing with the situation in the future and resolve to change their behavior so that the same issue won't reoccur.

These options are available, but children rarely use compromises without the guidance of their parents. In fact, most sibling-mediated conflicts from young childhood through adolescence end in no resolution or submission of one sibling to another rather than a true resolution involving issue or relationship compromise.

Even more generally, conflicts in the home—whether between children, parent and child, or spouses—usually are not resolved at all. This is true for sibling conflicts as well. Rarely do sibling conflicts involving children, toddlers to adolescents, end with compromise or reconciliation. Unresolved conflict for any family members provides fuel for more (and consistent) conflict in the future.

When children actually do manage to resolve their conflicts with each other, they rarely result in endings that favor the younger child. When parents ask children to work it out on their own, the older sibling often blames the younger sibling for the conflict and dominates the resolution process in his or her favor. In short, the younger sibling tends to lose repeatedly without parent intervention to help them express their feelings, goals, and interests. It's a dog-eat-dog world in the realm of sibling conflict without thoughtful parent intervention and support.

Workbook Questions:

- How do my children usually work out their conflicts with each other?

- How do my children's efforts to resolve conflict with

each other play out?

- If resolved, who usually "wins" the conflict?
- What are the pros and cons of my children working out their own solutions?
- What currently works in my home for resolving my children's conflicts?

Now that you understand the importance of the sibling relationships and the ways conflict happens between them, you can now look at your own thoughts, beliefs, and actions as a parent managing sibling conflict. In the next chapter, I focus on how parents approach their children who are in conflict. As you read, consider how your own parenting is similar to and different from typical family conflict patterns. Through this type of self-reflection on your parenting, you might gain some insight into what to change and what to keep from your conflict management tool bag.

Chapter 5 Summary

Siblings: A Near-Peer Relationship

Almost 80 percent of children in Western society grow up with a sibling.

Sibling Relationship Quality and Individual Social Development

Sibling relationship quality (warmth versus hostility) influences their social development over time.

Internalizing vs. Externalizing Stress and Negativity

Internalizing: The tendency for people to focus stress and negativity inwardly through social withdrawal, feelings of loneliness or guilt, not talking to or interacting with others, fearfulness, and not standing up for themselves.

Externalizing: The tendency for people to externalize stress and negativity by physical aggression, destruction of property, and more dramatic gestures such as running away from home.

Studies demonstrate that girls and women tend to struggle more with internalizing stress, while men and boys gravitate toward externalizing stress through outward acts of aggression or defiance.

Prosocial Behavior Development Possibilities through the Sibling Relationship

- Positive Engagement
- Cohesion
- Shared Experiences that Build Support
- Social and Emotional Understanding and Perspective Taking
- Emotion Regulation
- Behavioral Control
- Forming Neutral or Positive Attributions
- Problem Solving and Conflict Management

Overview of Sibling Conflict

- Frequency
- Topics of Conflict
- Conflict Tactics
- Possibilities for Sibling Conflict Endings (with or without parent intervention):
    - *Submission*—by a verbal or physical behavior, a child gives up his or her position.
    - *No Resolution*—the conflict ends with no resolution of the issue.
    - *Issue Compromise*—the children arrive at a

middle position or a new solution in which both children gain something.

- *Relationship Compromise*—the children decide to take each other's feelings into account when dealing with the situation in the future and resolve to change their patterns of interaction in such a way that this same issue would not reoccur.

CHAPTER 6

PATTERNS OF PARENT RESPONSES TO SIBLING CONFLICT

One day before trying to get some work done in the kitchen, I tried to anticipate the potential hazards of leaving my three young children in the adjacent family room. Realizing that I might need to protect my baby, Jack, from his curious older siblings, I placed him near the other kids' play area in his portable playpen. I felt confident that I could finish some tasks in the kitchen and not worry about Jack getting hurt by Emma and Ethan, who were three and two at the time, and I left the room.

Seconds later, Jack's loud cry brought me back to the play area, where I found Emma and Ethan throwing large toys onto Jack in his playpen. The mama bear in me reacted in anger. *Why would my children try to hurt their brother, my baby?* Given the dangers, I couldn't simply ignore their threatening behavior. Emma and Ethan were dropping large toys onto Jack in his playpen-turned prison.

This conflict demanded some teaching, some patience on my part, some structure and rules for the children, and some consistency in enforcing the rules. As a young mom, I believed that most parenting experts would agree that I needed to intervene swiftly because it involved physical danger to Jack. But when should I intervene in disagreements that don't involve physical danger, but relate to complicated, socio-psychological needs?

Following this episode with Jack, my mind returned to an earlier time when these questions about parent intervention into sibling conflict first surfaced.

As I gently unpacked more books from the cardboard boxes scattered on the ground of our spacious and empty basement, I was hopeful, excited, and full of visions of the many children that might someday fill our new (but older) home with activity and love. While nine months pregnant with my second child, Ethan, I was tired but happy to be putting my own home together after several weeks of living at my in-laws' home.

With the gentle light of an old lamp in the corner of the room, for a moment, I looked down at the parenting book I had recently received from my parents-in-law called *Children: The Challenge.* In my mind, I could hear my wise and loving mother-in-law's voice telling me that this book guided her and her husband in raising their children, as a how-to parenting reference.

To be honest, I hadn't read the other parenting books I had received at my daughter's shower a year or so earlier—except for the mission-critical *What to Expect When You're Expecting*. But, standing in that dimly lit room back in 2005, aware of my background as the daughter of divorced parents with two sets of divorced grandparents, I carefully read the back of Rudolf Dreikurs's famous 1964 bestselling handbook on raising children.

For a moment, my mind flashed to my own scattered childhood memories and considered the fact that my husband's parents so successfully raised eight loyal, hardworking, and obedient children that I chose to marry one of them after a decade of serious searching for the right partner in life. Not only was my husband a great person, but all his siblings seemed to have that salt-of-the-earth goodness about them.

As a social scientist and new young mother, I was skeptical about books that advocate parenting methodologies because many of them seemed very anecdotal and focused on one particular parenting trick or idea. But, I could not refute the fact that my in-laws raised wonderful children. So, in that moment, I decided to read the book despite my misgivings about parenting books in general.

In the whirlwind of life surrounding Ethan's birth, I managed to skim the book. Dreikurs firmly claims that all sibling bickering should be ignored so that children learn to respect their parents and work out their problems themselves. In his eyes, parent intervention (or attention) only increases children's appetite to engage in sibling conflict.

Dreikurs assumes that even a very young child will compete for a parents' attention using whatever means necessary, especially fighting with siblings. As I considered his arguments, I wondered if all sibling fighting really represented children's demands for attention from their parents.

Responding to Dreikurs's Call to Ignore Sibling Conflict

Since first reading Dreikurs, I have reflected on my more laissez-faire, but loving, childhood as the third of five children. I sometimes yearned for parental intervention to protect me, teach me, and comfort me amid ongoing sibling conflict. Even when my older brother received stern rebuke and discipline from my father, I pitied him and brought him small gifts afterward when he sat sulking in his room. Although I appreciated my father's intervening strongly on my behalf, I knew I could easily have been on the receiving end of such intense punishment. I feared getting in trouble for intended or unintended infractions, so I avoided many conflict situations.

During that time, I vowed never to spank or intimidate my own children. But as a parent, I soon learned that raising young children aggravated even the most patient corner of my soul. Eventually, while managing a household with three children under the age of three, I swallowed my pride and began studying parenting books. I realized, "Oh, so this is why people write these books—and others read them: parents actually need them!" Despite plans to raise my children differently—with more structure but also respectful teaching and explanation—I often felt overwhelmed (and even very angry) about all the screaming, the constancy of the conflict, and the overwhelming neediness of my young children. Sometimes, I am amazed that I've already made it through the early years and have actually become more patient, rather than more frustrated.

Despite believing that I couldn't ignore my children's fights, I didn't want to control them unnecessarily. With these conflicting feelings, I felt lost and didn't know which conflict resolution approaches worked or how I could use them effectively in my family. The ongoing sibling conflict I saw with my young children motivated me to find out which strategies work to curb conflict, but I also wanted to teach effective communication skills and strengthen our family relationships.

Given my hangups about Dreikurs's parenting ideas, I was pleased and surprised to find out about new child development studies about sibling conflict carried out by Dr. Hildy Ross and associated child development researchers at the University of Waterloo in Canada. Dr. Ross' studies on sibling conflict suggest that parent-led mediation may have a very positive impact on resolving sibling conflict and strengthening family relationships. Collaborative practices, such as mediation, balance concerns for children's autonomy and compliance with parental rules and guidelines. The result is greater compromise and reconciliation among siblings in conflict.

In this chapter, I explore the research that lays the foundation for parent-led mediation. First, I share how parents typically respond to conflict and identify the most effective ways to manage it. My goal is to encourage collaborative parenting approaches. While I focus on the power of collaboration, please realize that it is a tool to supplement the four general conflict approaches you may already be using.

Understanding Our Approaches to Handling Sibling Conflict

Just as children use different languages to communicate their thoughts, feelings, and ideas with each other, parents use different conflict approaches to handle children's negative interactions. As I show you in this chapter, some approaches are more effective than others. I remember a day during my road trip to Canada with my kids when I had several opportunities to "study" how I handle sibling conflict.

One cloudy summer day, I was several days into a solo parent road trip driving my children from Denver, Colorado, to Banff, Alberta, Canada. As we approached the grandiose and complex entrance to Banff National Park, I felt tense and alert, but highly distracted by my children's fighting in the back of the car. I had tried to ignore the bickering for several minutes in a show of great parental patience, but I finally lost it when I missed the entrance into Banff. I pulled the car over and blamed the kids for our failure to enter the park correctly (notice how I had missed the turn, but blamed them for that failure?).

At that point, I was beyond seeking explanation from

the kids, but assigned blame without justification. In their own way, each of my five children reacted to my outburst, crying, looking down, or becoming silent. I had achieved my immediate goal of silence so that I could backtrack to the entrance and find my way. But, I had distanced myself from my children by asserting power in the moment, a strategy that wouldn't likely work in the future as they grew older and matured.

I don't expect that I'll be perfectly calm and composed in every parenting moment, but in retrospect, I realize how I could have better anticipated problems and enlisted the kids' support in this anxiety-producing situation. Unfortunately, I ignored their fighting until I couldn't deal with it anymore. I now see how I could have handled the situation differently. I could have taken time to reflect rather than assigning blame and using my waning parental authority to control the independent, though young, human beings in my care.

As parents, we often react because we are busy, tired, or out of ideas. Maybe we were raised a certain way that was effective for our generation, but doesn't seem to work with our children. Whatever the reason, we use a variety of approaches to handle our conflicts and our children's conflicts with each other.

Some approaches are more effective than others to resolve conflicts and build relationships over the long term. We can't apply the "right" approach perfectly in every conflict situation, but we can be more deliberate about how we respond to children's conflicts and do so with greater confidence if we apply better tools, strategies, and perspective.

To prepare for applying mediation principles in your home, it helps to understand what research reveals about the outcomes you can expect from different approaches. As child development researchers tackle the task of studying family conflict dynamics, recent child-centric studies suggest that certain parent interventions are more effective than some go-to approaches that parents typically use.

I understand the constraints parents face in daily life, which make it challenging to manage children's behavior effectively. But, more collaborative intervention benefits children, both immediately and over the long term in socio-emotional development.

Collaborative intervention, rather than ignoring, punishing, or assigning blame, paves the way for incredible social development gains for children. In addition, methods like mediation strengthen family relationships over time as these collaborative behaviors become habitual.

Parent Approaches to Sibling Conflict

All parents deal with ongoing sibling conflict to lesser or greater degrees. They often say that sibling conflict represents a major parenting concern. As with other types of familial conflict, most sibling conflict goes unresolved despite parents' desire for quick reconciliation. This lack of resolution represents a critical deficit in children's capacity to manage differences that matter throughout their lives.

Parents would probably prefer to eliminate all conflict in the home, but research suggests that sibling conflict in moderate doses offers an opportunity for children to learn critical problem-solving skills, perspective taking, and empathy. But to gain this benefit, parents need to engage more fully in the resolution process than research indicates we prefer. Researchers have identified how often our ideas about parenting differ from what we practice in our daily lives.

How Do Parents Typically Respond to Sibling Conflict?

Parents often emphasize that each parent is different, like each child is different. We have unique features as individual human beings. But parents also experience many similar (or shared) tendencies that have been closely studied in recent years. This research includes overarching patterns of parents in Western society and provides important insight into the shared parenting tendencies and experiences that arise despite our unique experiences as parents in our individual homes.

While it's difficult to untangle all the factors that contribute to our common parenting tendencies, research shows that parent intervention in sibling conflict matters to the results. Although the type of parent intervention also matters, many negative social outcomes are associated with parents failing to intervene in or ignoring their children's more hostile conflicts with each other.

From research by the late Dr. Lisa Perozynski and Dr. Laurie Kramer, we learn that most parents express confidence in the effectiveness of more child-centered approaches that involve listening, reflecting, and seeking collaborative solutions to resolve sibling conflicts. Yet, in everyday life, parents often ignore their children's conflicts. In fact, in research settings, parents chose to ignore their children's conflicts most of the time, hoping the kids would work it out themselves or lose interest in the conflict. One study even suggested that parents opt to ignore sibling conflicts three times as often as any other response.

Compounding avoidance tactics, the same research suggests that when parents do intervene in their children's more intense conflicts, they rarely provide the structure children need to communicate with one another or work out issues on their own. Most parents intervene as judges or punishers, assigning blame without focusing on the children's perspectives, thoughts, and emotions. While these are general tendencies, they don't determine your parenting behavior; you can choose different approaches to conflict in your family, and I'll show you how.

Workbook Questions:

- How do I usually resolve my children's verbal conflicts?

- How do I usually resolve my children's physical conflicts?

- Do my strategies differ in different types of conflicts (e.g., personal property, rules of fairness, family privileges, teasing, physical vs. verbal assaults)?

- Which conflict management approaches are working for me and your family?

- Which conflict management approaches need improvement or new ideas?

Example of a Parent in Action:

Several years ago, I recorded the following experience in which I questioned my parenting strategies. As you read about my experience, consider my good intentions, but also my lack of preparation for the potential conflicts I encountered with my kids.

The Five-Dollar Garage Sale Disaster

One day I threw a child-sized motorized vehicle in the garbage can. It worked great, and the children loved it while they drove it, but they fought over it because there was only one vehicle—that's all they had at the garage sale where I bought it for five dollars. I told Amy and Ben they needed to share it, but during the brief four hours of joint ownership they fought over it constantly.

During the first thirty minutes, they both sat on it, back to back, screaming and hitting each other. Ben was indignant that Amy had been hitting him, but he wouldn't get off of the car.

Despite their heavy screaming and rage, I managed to get them to sit on the garage floor and "discuss" how they could both ride the vehicle in a fair way. We talked about who would go first and where that person would get off so the next person could drive. Somehow, we managed to drive and walk to the park without screaming or hitting.

As we approached the main playground area, I could see one little boy eyeing the vehicle with envy. Since I knew his father, I offered to let the boy take it for a spin, but the father seemed to sense the possibility for conflict and politely declined.

After the heat had gotten to the kids and we decided to drive and walk home, the contentions began again. Ben screamed as Amy drove farther than he thought reasonable in his four-year-old mind. He ran after her and stood in front of her.

Frustrated after a full day loaded with conflict, I picked up the five-dollar garage sale treasure and placed it in the garbage. I realized I had a choice: continue to negotiate the conflict or get rid of the source.

Thirty minutes after disposing of the vehicle, I wondered if it might be a good tool to help them negotiate with each other, but I wasn't willing to put in the time and effort to work through the conflict. In this case, I had to weigh my other priorities and family needs before I took it on again. Besides, I had until the next Tuesday (garbage day) to make up my mind. Several years after the fact, Ben and Amy don't even remember the vehicle or that I threw it away.

Perhaps my five-dollar garage sale disaster has stirred memories of trying to settle your children's arguments and your less-than-satisfying parenting moments. All parents experience moments like these. But, we gain insight from thinking about choices in light of child development and psychology research. Parents should consider what research can teach us about child development, conflict resolution, and mediation. Hopefully, my related stories and examples help you remember that parenting is not easy, that there are lots of moving parts, and that holding ourselves to impossible standards doesn't help anyone.

Three Main Parent Strategies for Dealing with Children's Conflicts

While parents use a variety of tactics, tones of voice, rewards, punishments, threats, demands, and so forth to manage children's conflicts, parenting responses fall into three broad categories of conflict management strategies, which include the following:

- Passive Nonintervention Strategies (Ignoring)
- Control Strategies
- Child-Centered Strategies

In this next section, I briefly highlight definitions, explanations, and examples of each category. I follow this section with research on and questions about parent intervention (and nonintervention) in sibling conflict. Throughout this chapter, I offer the opportunity to pause and answer questions about your own experience in managing your children's conflicts so you can understand your own parenting habits and beliefs.

Passive Nonintervention Strategies (Ignoring)

Passive nonintervention means that parents don't intervene or get involved in children's conflicts for whatever reason. Parents either ignore children's fighting altogether or don't involve themselves enough to change the course of the conflict in any significant way. This often takes the form of telling children to work out the conflict on their own.

In research published in 1999 by the late Dr. Lisa Perozynski and Dr. Laurie Kramer, parents choose to ignore their children's fighting three times more often than they intervene. They usually don't provide coaching or structure to help siblings in resolving conflicts on their own.

Parents have many reasons for not intervening in sibling conflict, but overusing this strategy comes with potentially high costs for parents and children. Data about parental nonintervention suggests that parents often don't take the opportunity to teach children critical lifelong conflict management skills, which are best learned in early childhood and through our most significant, intimate relationships. Some less than desirable outcomes of not intervening in sibling conflict include the following:

- Fewer conflicts are resolved.
- If resolved, conflicts are less likely to result in compromise.
- Conflicts tend to have winners and losers.
- Older, more powerful siblings tend to "win" the conflict.

- Older, more powerful siblings tend to blame younger siblings much more often than in collaborative settings, which increases power differences between siblings and limits older siblings' use of empathy skills and perspective taking.

Research on the failure to intervene in children's conflicts suggests that parents should consider other options for handling frequent and intense conflicts among children. Ignoring conflict sometimes works well, and parents might believe that letting children work out conflicts on their own is necessary for their development. But, the research clearly states that most sibling conflict does not get resolved effectively by siblings, and if it is resolved, the older siblings usually dominate the resolution process and the outcomes.

I recall the first night I allowed Emma to cry herself to sleep as a six-month-old baby. I swaddled her up tight in her blanket and laid her gently in her crib. At six months, I knew that she could learn to sleep through the night if I could bear to hear her cry for me without responding. After shutting her door for the night, I lasted about twenty minutes before I couldn't stand hearing her cries for attention.

Before I went into Emma's room to calm her, my husband told me I needed to get out of hearing range so I wouldn't feel drawn to go help her. He felt that she could learn to sleep on her own if I would remove my presence so that she knew she needed to fall asleep.

After about fifty minutes, she fell asleep. I felt relieved, but also guilty that I had not responded to her call. Because she did learn to go to sleep by herself after that evening, I realized that sometimes I needed to ignore her need to help her grow. This impression that ignoring might be necessary for child development returns on occasion when I deal with ongoing conflict demands with my children.

When I face sibling conflict situations, I ask whether my intervention will be useful or not. Despite trusting that nonintervention might be useful, I temper this idea with the understanding that some skills require more parent intervention and that children won't naturally develop these skills on their own.

Parents should gradually withdraw their scaffolding of conflict communication processes as children age, mature, and gain mastery. First, we must assume the role of communications teacher before we expect trained, skilled communicators. Children are not always equipped with the developmental skills and know-how to negotiate social interactions successfully without our support and explicit skills training.

Control Strategies

Control strategies include threats, demands, and even physical coercion to force children to obey the parent's will. Parents may withhold privileges, introduce rewards or punishments for behavior, and, assert parental authority to make children comply with certain demands. In a positive sense, parents may use control strategies to suggest, endorse, or enforce decisions upon our children. But too often, parents apply this strategy inappropriately, especially with our older children who grow ever more capable of reasoning, empathy, and perspective taking.

As I reflect on control strategies, I'm reminded of an exhausting day nearly eight years ago when I tried to control my toddler son's behavior using forceful tactics. I recall the following details with some embarrassment, but also appreciation for what I learned from this experience.

While holding my two-year old son's door closed, I yelled, "You're going to time out! I'm going to hold the door to your room until you learn to stay there when I ask you to." My son was pulling on the inside knob with all his might to release himself from his benign prison cell. The other two children were nearby in the hallway crying for my attention—I couldn't hold either of them because I needed both hands to hold the door closed. The time out seemed to do nothing for either of us. I was exhausted, angry, and intellectually stumped. I wondered silently, "What truly works for me and my child? How can I teach him to obey generally fair family rules without crushing his beautiful spirit?"

As we added two more children to bring our total to five under the age of six, I experienced greater pressure to somehow control my household of preschoolers and toddlers. During the hazy fog of their early lives, I cannot forget the poignant advice an unmarried, childless aunt gave me about my child-rearing practices. She had noticed the many conflicts we experienced, particularly with one extra boisterous and disobedient child. As the owner of several prize-winning dogs, she looked me squarely in the eyes and told me that I needed to treat this child like she would one of her dogs. I needed to be very clear and precise about my commands, then be consistent with rewards and punishments.

Her words stung me like a whip. Though I remained somewhat unfazed on the outside, I felt ready either to cry or scream inside. I had heard this brand of parenting advice from many different corners. I had felt it in the gaze of parents at the playground, through comments from relatives who had never experienced this kind of rambunctious behavior, and in the gentle words of friends whose children calmly followed their directions without screaming or intense impetuousness. These outside sources pushed this unrelenting message: Perhaps medication or a strong dose of Love and Logic principles, parenting techniques developed in the late 1970s by Jim Fay and Dr. Foster W. Cline, could cure our home of its conflicts and emotional outbursts? Despite suggestions from others, I was determined to find parenting methods that involved more than coercion and control.

There are appropriate times to use control strategies—particularly in time-sensitive situations involving personal safety. But, when parents rely too exclusively on control strategies, they push children away and miss out on opportunities to strengthen family ties and prepare children for greater independence. Parents need to encourage, not force, children to develop problem-solving, empathy, and perspective-taking skills in an environment of trust and respect. We must not underestimate the importance of *how we teach*, even if we strongly believe that *what we teach* is valuable.

Child-Centered Strategies

Child-centered parenting strategies focus on children's thoughts and feelings, but also their development of independent problem-solving skills. Rather than resolve conflicts for children, parents focus on guiding children through conflict resolution so that they build social skills while working through issues with their siblings.

When parents use child-centered strategies, they need more time to explore children's thoughts and emotions. They also must demonstrate emotional stability so they can calmly discuss conflict topics without blaming or accusing children of wrongdoing. Parents take the long view of development with this method: Time spent up front to directly teach and model collaborative methods of listening, empathizing, and perspective taking will pay off with more mature behaviors as children learn to master their thoughts, emotions, and resulting actions. Mastering these skills of listening, empathizing, and perspective prepares children for more constructive conflict management.

Through child-centered strategies, parents focus on more than obedience to demands. Greater cooperation may be a natural outcome of a more collaborative approach because parents show children that their thoughts and ideas matter and that they are capable of solving problems themselves. In short, parents try to furnish as much opportunity as children's temperaments, skills, and development allow for independence in social interaction. They buffer and support children in resolving their conflicts with each other, but also focus on preparing them for gradual independence by building their self-confidence based on experience and skill building.

Outcomes of Collaborative Parent Intervention in Sibling Conflict

When parents use collaborative parent interventions with sibling conflict, typical outcomes include the following:

- Reduction in tension in children and their families
- Upholding of family rules of fairness
- Decrease in conflict intensity
- Increase in children's use of reasoning
- Development of children's other-oriented reasoning skills
- Encouragement of more mature conflict behaviors in children

While parents often have the ability to quickly perceive the ins and outs of their children's conflicts, parents benefit their children most by helping them recognize and practice collaborative problem-solving skills mostly on their own with some parent guidance.

For example, one late afternoon, I encountered a conflict between my daughter Amy and her sister, Emma, that involved jealousy between my youngest daughter and her friend during a playdate. I could have tried to resolve this conflict solely on my own, but I decided to take the time to teach the girls how to handle it themselves.

During the playdate, my older daughter, Emma, treated Amy's six-year-old best friend, Kristen, like a queen. Emma carried Amy's friend around on her back, helped her with dinner, answered her beck and call, and showed considerable empathy for this cute, blond-haired girl.

Midway through dinner, Amy complained that Emma had interfered in her playdate. I could sense that it wasn't so much the interference that was bothering Amy, but Emma's focus on serving and helping her friend. Rather than let this pattern escalate into true conflict (nonintervention) or tell Amy to knock it off (control), I intervened, privately, with Emma.

I took Emma aside in another room and explained to her how Amy might have felt jealous about her special treatment of Kristen. First, I praised Emma for being such a fun and kind "big sister" to Kristen, who has struggled at school and with friends. I explained how I understood the difficulty of maintaining fairness among her brothers and sisters. But, I also warned Emma about showing preferential treatment to Kristen, especially in front of Amy, because it created feelings of jealousy and anger. I asked her to share her thoughts and feelings about what I had said. She understood the dilemma and seemed ready to adapt her behavior to prevent a conflict with Amy.

Emma responded positively to the discussion and my overt teaching. She understood what I was trying to teach because we talked it through with a focus on not only Amy's feelings, but Emma's as well.

As parents, we encounter all kinds of conflict situations

that involve our children. Some conflicts are still brewing in the background, while others are going full steam. We can choose whether and when to teach important skills and ideas. The truth is I don't always have the energy to intervene in the optimal way, but in this case, I intervened with the proper focus on my children's thoughts and feelings so my daughter received my message without defensiveness or anger.

Workbook Questions:

- What types of conflict resolution strategies do I find most effective and why?
- When am I most likely to ignore my children's conflicts?
- When am I most likely to use control strategies?
- When am I most likely to use child-centered strategies?
- When are the best times for me to apply each of the conflict resolution strategies?
- Which conflict resolution strategies do I feel most confident using?
- How effective do I feel at resolving my children's conflicts?

To Intervene or Not in Sibling Conflict

Before parents decide how to help their children resolve a conflict, they first must address one central question: Should they intervene in children's conflicts?

Parents have a wide variety of reasons for not intervening. As I mentioned in earlier chapters, many parents were raised to believe that getting involved in sibling conflict only feeds children's appetite for more conflict. Parents may assume that growing maturity and increased verbal expression mean children can work out conflicts themselves. Others have a high tolerance for sibling conflict and assume that kids just fight with each other and they'll grow out of it. Parents might also believe that they turned out all right without much parent intervention in conflicts with brothers or sisters, so why should they intervene with their own kids?

What Does the Research Say about Parent Intervention?

We can learn a lot about the influence of parent intervention in sibling conflict from various recent studies of hundreds of families trying to resolve sibling conflict. While intervening with control strategies are necessary and appropriate in many situations, thoughtful, child-centered parent intervention supports the most significant benefits for children. These strategies decrease the likelihood of continued sibling conflict while reducing the tension between fighting children and upholding family rules of fairness. Besides decreasing conflict intensity, constructive parent intervention supports children's ability to reason, which facilitates positive conflict resolution.

While research results from studies by Dr. Hildy Ross, Dr. Michal Perlman, and Dr. Afshan Siddiqui suggest that child-focused solutions are ideal, it is typical for parents to intervene in their children's more intense conflicts from a position of authority and not provide the structure for children to communicate or work out issues on their own. Failing to help children explore their emotions related to sibling conflicts is a missed opportunity to help children. Despite the potential to provide different types of support, parents rarely coach their children in applying effective communication skills and methods in their conflicts with others. We either involve ourselves as a judge or remove ourselves and become a passive observer or nonparticipant.

Researchers focused on parent-led mediation, such as Dr. Hildy Ross, Dr. Afshan Siddiqui, Dr. Julie Smith, and Dr. Marysia J. Lazinski, have shown that when parents either ignore or intervene as judges in their children's conflicts with each other, they can expect the following results:

- Less discussion of emotions or interests related to the conflict or relationship
- Less focus on strengthening of relationships
- Kids are more likely to make demands and offer justifications for their own positions
- Children accuse and insult one another more often (which is nearly absent in mediation groups)
- Unbalanced power situations
- More win-lose outcomes
- Fewer compromise outcomes
- Parents are more likely to resolve conflicts for the kids
- Older siblings are more likely to blame younger siblings for the conflict

These research results support the idea that typical approaches to sibling conflict don't help us achieve our ultimate goals of unity and positive relationships within the family. As we explore what research tells us about sibling conflict management, it's important that we carefully consider our own habits and beliefs and modify them as needed.

Research indicates that both mothers and fathers are more likely to intervene in their children's more intense conflicts, especially those that involve physical aggression. Parents intervene more often in circumstances with an older brother and a younger sister, like my situations with Ethan and Amy. In terms of the positive influence of mothers in sibling conflict management, in one 1997 study by Dr. Carla Herrera and Dr. Judy Dunn, researchers found that when mothers intervened in sibling conflicts using reasoning that focused on understanding the perspectives of others, their children were more likely to use other-focused reasoning when resolving conflicts with their friends. In fact, a mother's use of other-focused reasoning is more strongly correlated with her child's later conflict management style than with the child's early argument style as a youth.

Once parents choose how they will manage their children's conflict in a given situation (i.e., passive nonintervention, control, or child-centered strategies), they typically follow their initial choice and use additional tactics from the same type of strategy as needed. These decisions rest heavily on whom parents' think is to blame among the siblings. When parents assume that one child is to blame for a conflict, they intervene with a heavier hand and are more likely to employ a control strategy with the "guilty" child. But, if parents are unsure who is to blame for the conflict, they use more child-centered strategies that involve active listening, reflecting, other-oriented reasoning, and collaboration.

Research by Dr. Nina Howe and Dr. Holly Recchia of the University of Concordia reveals some information that parents should take to heart if they find that they assign blame to one child regularly. Sibling relationships are more likely to be conflictual and less friendly when parents treat their children differently with varying amounts of *positive* emotional interaction, responsiveness, control, discipline, and intrusiveness between the two children. If children view the differences in treatment by parents as unfair, there may be negative effects in the children's relationships with each other and their parents.

Workbook Questions:

- When do I intervene in my children's conflicts?

- What types of conflict situations motivate me to engage in resolving the conflict?

- How do my children usually respond to me when I intervene?

- Why do I intervene the way that I do?

Conclusion

Although we may resist intervening in children's conflicts with each other because of time constraints, fatigue, anger, a lack of confidence, habit, or a lack of skills, we cannot underestimate the positive influence that child-centered intervention strategies have in their lives. Rather than sweep sibling conflict under the rug, we know that parent intervention focused on children and their thoughts and feelings provides a vital opportunity for them to expand their social learning and development and reduce sibling conflict intensity and frequency in the long run.

As we nourish children's relationships with each other through focused guidance and direct teaching of collaborative problem solving, we prepare them to successfully manage the many relationships and conflicts they encounter throughout their entire lives.

With this foundation, I want to share one promising collaborative conflict resolution method: parent-led mediation. With parent-led mediation, we unlock the power of a child-centered parent intervention linked with problem-solving, empathy, and perspective-taking skill building that will benefit our children (and us) for a lifetime.

Chapter 6 Summary

Responding to Dreikurs's Call to Ignore Sibling Conflict

Current research shows the benefits of child-centered parent intervention for managing sibling conflict, which contradicts previous statements by Dreikurs that parents should ignore all sibling conflict.

Understanding Our Parenting Approaches to Handling Sibling Conflict

Most parents express confidence in the effectiveness of more child-centered approaches that involve listening, reflecting, and seeking collaborative solutions to resolve sibling conflicts. But, in everyday life, parents often ignore their children's conflicts.

When parents do intervene, primarily as judges or punishers, in their children's more intense conflicts, they rarely provide the structure children need to communicate with one another or work out issues on their own.

Three Main Parental Strategies for Dealing with Children's Conflicts

- *Passive Nonintervention (Ignoring)*: Passive nonintervention means that we don't intervene or get involved in children's conflicts.

- *Control Strategies*: Control parenting strategies employ threats, demands, and even physical coercion to try to force our children to obey our will.

- *Child-Centered Strategies*: Child-centered strategies focus on children's thoughts, feelings, and their development of independent problem-solving skills.

To Intervene or Not Intervene in Sibling Conflict

New research explores the positive effect of parent intervention in sibling conflict. The research focuses on what is effective and how often parents use the three main parenting strategies of passive nonintervention (ignoring), control, and child-centered.

CHAPTER 7

ANALYZING PARENT CONFLICT MANAGEMENT APPROACHES IN CONTEXT

As parents, we often know what we should do to help our kids with conflicts, but we don't always succeed in carrying out our perfect parenting plans. In this chapter, I explore a specific scenario of conflict contagion among my family members using a specific acronym: TEACH ME. I explain the acronym in detail within this chapter so you can apply it in your own family.

As you experiment with the TEACH ME steps, understand that you'll experience challenges and successes. Conflicts that begin with children may ignite parent conflict behavior. In the same way, research demonstrates that spousal or parental conflict may arouse conflict tendencies in children. As you read, try to identify potential environmental factors, conflict management strategies, or beliefs that may have escalated conflict in various relationships. From this passage, you can see that as a family, we are a work in progress!

A couple years ago, I really dreaded Tuesdays. I'm sure my children dreaded them too. In particular, there were two Tuesdays that forced me to seriously reflect on how to improve my parenting, especially with kids in conflict with each other.

Despite a calm morning, one Tuesday afternoon, once the children had hopped off the bus after school, I stood in the family room and called out directions like a drill sergeant preparing for a battle. I reminded Jack and Ethan to throw on their Cub Scout shirts, called out to Amy and Emma to get their violins and music bag, and made sure that Ben remembered to bring his piano solfeggio worksheet so he could complete it during the violin lessons. I complained because, once again, I ended up grabbing the violins and music bag and lugged it all out to the car along with my purse and car keys.

After a short drive to drop Ethan and Jack off at the church, we zoomed up the road to arrive a minute or two late for violin lessons. Amy and Emma argued about who would go first with Ms. J, their teacher. I vacillated between their opposing desires and opted to intervene so that Emma would go first for a change, even though she usually wanted to start by doing homework while Amy had her lesson. Emma had to accept a change to our usual routine because Amy didn't like going first either.

Emma began her lesson, but Ben and Amy kept opening the door and interrupting the lesson. Neither younger child would stay in the basement because they were scared of the vast space and darkness. Fighting commenced with the two wrestling with each other at the door. Within seconds, I abandoned my required post as the Suzuki mom in Emma's lesson to calm my two youngest children.

But, they didn't not calm down. I threatened to take away their computer privileges for the day, then laid down the law by confirming that I had, indeed, taken away their computer privileges. At this point, I sat in the dimly lit living room, and all heck broke loose; my children screamed in aggravation from the unjust punishment I quickly imposed. For some reason, I forgot to take them to the basement during their outbursts and chose instead to calmly hold them in my arms to keep them close as they screamed and writhed. The house was quiet otherwise, but I imagined that Ms. J's teenage children were disturbed by my children's expressions of fury.

Before we left that evening, I felt embarrassed and apologized to Ms. J. I hoped that the next Tuesday would be better. I was determined that it would be better, but, as you may have expected, I couldn't always control the elements that determined such success. For some reason, even after years of toddler tantrums, I believed that I could leave these emotional outbursts behind. But, not so.

The next Tuesday, I arrived with the same three children plus Jack, who didn't have Cub Scouts that week. Upon welcoming us into her home, our teacher reminded us of the tantrum of the prior week and stated that we could not disturb her children again; we had to retreat to the basement.

I made a joke about the behavior, but there was no reciprocating smile of approval, only the admonition not to repeat the previous week's offenses. I felt shaken by the reminder, yet this was a new Tuesday, and I was optimistic.

I decided to hang out in the basement with my three youngest children while Emma completed her lesson without me. Given his older age, I was surprised by Jack's angry outburst at the foosball table. He screamed as if his finger has been cut off. But it was a loss of a different kind that had upset him. He was losing to his younger brother, Ben, because of an accidental swipe of the ball into his own goal; consequently, Jack had unleashed his hostility.

Determined not to be embarrassed again, I ran over to the foosball table and demanded that he quit crying. As my demands for him to quit screaming (and embarrassing us, especially me) went unheeded, I felt a surge of rage and lack of control. I picked Jack up, and with intense sternness, I commanded that he be quiet.

This unleashing of parental indignation had absolutely no effect. I recognized the familiar sting of my disabused pride as I carried him to a couch on the far side of the room and explained how furious I was. Soon, I recognized the source of my hostility: I felt embarrassed and ashamed. I, the great mediator and conflict resolution specialist, could not control my son. Here in this violin teacher's basement, I demanded immediate reconciliation, but my child demanded autonomy and freedom to express his frustrations about losing to his younger brother.

We sat for a few moments in a somewhat quiet standoff. Once again, I was reminded that no matter the pressure of feeling judged for my children's behavior, I could not coerce good conduct, especially with my rapidly maturing son. He had goals as well, which differed from mine, especially in that moment. He did not want to lose the foosball game and wasn't about to back down from fighting with his brother about the outcome.

Reviewing Conflict Experiences in Light of Conflict Resolution Skills and Training

As you read about this series of conflicts with my children, you may have recognized that one conflict ignited many others in a progressively heated way. Specific environmental factors, basic beliefs about parenting, and conflict management strategies created and escalated many conflicts during these busy Tuesdays. Even before we arrived at the violin lesson, my children and I had already been fanning the flames of conflict with overscheduling, a lack of downtime, failure to solidify a fair decision about who would go first, and a lack of proper childcare for my younger children who need adult supervision.

With this background, I include environmental factors, communication skills, and parental beliefs in my review to understand how to de-escalate rather than fuel family conflict. The goal is to resolve, not just diminish or delay, conflict in any given moment by applying approaches based on all our needs.

Once I had some time to reflect upon these unfolding events, I realized how I had set my family up to experience conflict and stress and failed to achieve our ultimate, long-term goals of harmony, growth, and love for each other. But, through reviewing this experience, I can use the insight I've gained to modify factors within my control and support my family's ultimate peace and benefit. In short, I can actively take several steps to contain the flame of conflict with proper understanding, planning, and skill building for both myself and my children. I will apply the TEACH ME steps to the conflict scenario to explore *parent behavior* with sibling conflicts. Later, I will use the same acronym to explain the steps of *parent-led mediation*.

Test Expectations
Establish Patterns
Anticipate Conflict
Choose to be Proactive
Help Kids as Needed
Mediate
Enjoy the Process

T—Test Expectations

Understanding and Modifying Parental Expectations

In a highly competitive society where we emphasize early academic, athletic, musical, and other achievement for children, parents often lead exhausted lives. Out of genuine caring for the development of our children, we impose considerable expectations and stress on not only them, but also ourselves to ensure they do not miss out on key experiences.

Unlike generations past, we rely more and more on the nuclear family or hired help rather than our community and extended family to provide what we believe to be mission-critical development experiences for our children. While many of us once rode bikes around town, played in the park, and sold lemonade unsupervised on the street corner, today many of us spend countless after-school hours shuttling our kids through traffic to various activities and clubs that require extensive parent participation, money, and time commitments.

Become Proactive Rather Than Reactive

Parents often make decisions about their children's activities, but feel guilty about what they don't choose to do, such as missing out on the swim team because of a family road trip or choosing basketball instead of soccer. Parents are inundated with choices, and it feels as if we react to the demands of school, extended family, and societal expectations, rather than being proactive in setting the priorities, pace, and tone for our personal and family lives.

In short, we feel we must respond to demands, rather than actively creating our lives according to our family's values and purposes. Our expectations—that is, what we expect ourselves and our children to accomplish in the same twenty-four hours—have skyrocketed out of proportion to what most of us can reasonably handle on a given day.

Engulfed in our culture of achievement and the natural desires for my children's enrichment, I hold these same high expectations for my children's development and growth. While I had a very casual experience learning piano as a child, as a nanny during my college years, I witnessed how one family put intense effort into raising great musicians through dedicated daily practice and parent involvement. Based on these experiences, I hoped to offer my children greater musical experiences than I had enjoyed as a child.

I started piano lessons at eight years old, but I intended for each of my children to choose an instrument by the time they were six. Currently, my girls are learning the violin, Jack has picked up the cello, and Ben and Ethan play the piano. In no way do I liken myself to an Amy Chua's "Tiger Mom," but my choices are influenced by my high hopes for my children and society's push towards early and intense child participation in extracurricular activities.

Given my high expectations for my children, I chose a violin teacher who used a technique to develop high-level talent and interest. I believed this teacher would provide the opportunity for my children to excel if they desired it. I have struggled with my inner conflict of wanting to provide a fantastic musical learning opportunity while adapting my expectations to my children's current skill level and motivation. This conflict between my expectations and my children's desires were the source of most of the initial conflict we experienced before we even got into the car for the first of these Tuesday lessons.

Workbook Questions:

- What are my expectations for my children's academic, musical, and athletic development?
- Are there any conflicts with my spouse or children about my expectations? If so, what are the main conflicts I experience?
- How do I manage my own expectations, as well as my partner's and children's expectations?

Consider That Stress May Signal the Need for Change

In retrospect, I realized that the stress was a signal to reflect and possibly change what we were doing and how. After almost a year of stressful Tuesdays (and writing about it), I asked myself if I could imagine any alternatives to our current patterns. Given time to consider, right away I imagined hiring a different teacher who could come to our house on a different day, finding childcare for my younger kids, or choosing not to participate in all the violin lessons. Stress does not always mean that we need to make a change, but as we become aware of stress in ourselves and our children, we may develop more stable family patterns over the long term.

Parents as Limited Resources

To provide stability within our families, parents might benefit from seeing themselves as limited resources rather than limitless sources of energy, wisdom, and patience. Let me explain.

Several years ago, as I was escorting my five kids (then ranging in age from one to six) from the swimming pool— believe me, I was done with the pool at that moment—a friend approached me with a very poignant question. She is a poised and rather sophisticated child psychologist and mother of four young children. After confiding in me how angry she sometimes gets at her kids, she leaned in and asked me, "How are you not angry all the time with all your kids?"

I was surprised by her honesty about the anger she often felt from trying to manage her four young children. I responded with the following:

"I do get angry, but in recent years, I have come to realize that I am a limited resource. I have only so much energy, patience, intellect, and imagination to get through each day. Because of that, I plan my day around what I can reasonably accomplish without losing my wits.

"If I know I usually get cranky and angry around din- nertime, that's when I put on a show for my kids. I know that one of my sons will run out the automatic doors at the library, so we just don't go there right now. I can't handle it. Basically, I plan my day around what I can reasonably accom- plish without getting mad."

To some, treating ourselves as limited resources may seem like a cop-out, but when we recognize our limitations and needs as people and parents, we set the tone for daily life, especially with young children who depend on not only our help with physical tasks, but on our general mood and attitude for emotional stability. We set up our children's expectations for their own lives by how we pattern our own. What will our children inherit from us about priorities and stable life patterns?

Workbook Questions:

- When do I get the most stressed? Certain times of day? Certain days of the week? Around the holidays?
- How do I manage myself as a limited parenting resource?
- How could I change my life and expectations to reduce personal and familial stress?

Respect That Children and Their Developmental Skills Are Not Interchangeable

Even parents who don't have five children may recognize a tendency to treat children as if their developmental skills and abilities are interchangeable with their siblings. For example, I could have left Emma alone to finish her homework in Ms. J's basement, but my youngest children, Ben and Amy, were not mature enough to supervise themselves. I left them to their own devices so I could participate in Emma's violin lesson. I needed a backup plan that respected Ben and Amy's development by providing the assistance of an adult or older child.

I also assumed that Jack, who rarely attends violin with us and seldom plays foosball with his younger brother, could adapt quickly to the new environment and competitive situation. I assumed too much—that Jack could quickly forget the bruising of his ego as he lost a foosball game to his younger brother and that he could muster the social savvy to quiet his crying when he became frustrated. Lacking the experience of the prior week's embarrassment, Jack inherited my frustration with the other two kids who had caused problems before. As a newcomer to the situation, Jack's conflict behavior took on greater meaning (and intensity) than it might have otherwise.

As parents, we should not assume that one child's skills and development are interchangeable with that of another. An older child may have a harder time handling a new situation than a younger sibling—or a brother versus a sister. We need to take them for who they are based on their personality, temperament, and skill set in a particular environmental situation.

Workbook Questions:

- Do I ever act as if my children's skills are interchangeable?
- If so, what effect does that attitude and practice have on me and my children?
- What skills do my children need to develop that I might focus on in the near future?

E—Establish Patterns

Avoid Overscheduling

With high expectations for child achievement, I had overscheduled myself and my children. You may have noticed that on Tuesday everyone felt stressed even before heading to Cub Scouts and violin lessons. With little or no downtime after school, I urged my children into the car and off to more organized activities that did not provide true play or relaxation.

Even as an adult, I felt stressed knowing what lay before us in terms of driving, encouraging, motivating, resolving, feeding, and disciplining my kids as necessary. In the concentration of activity, we left little room for social learning or true engagement outside of the activities at hand. My choice to get involved in Cub Scouts, violin, piano, soccer, and everything else hinges on the belief that these activities will benefit my children. Most of the time, I accept the stress of such a life because I believe there is no other way around it. But, we do have choice in all daily activities. This experience of overscheduling caused me to make some significant scheduling changes that I will discuss at the end of this chapter.

Workbook Questions:

- In what ways is my family overscheduled?
- What kind of family life would I like to create?
- How could I modify my family schedule so that I can proactively create the family patterns I want for my

home life?

A–Anticipate Conflict

Plan for Conflicts When Possible

While I did not fully anticipate Amy and Ben's initial outburst on the first Tuesday, I did fail to reflect on the risk of leaving Ben and Amy without supervision during Emma's lesson. I assumed they could handle being alone, but I could have prepared better by allowing Emma to do her lesson alone with her teacher. While not ideal in the Suzuki method, as a limited resource, I could have determined my abilities and my children's level of development, and accepted a less-than-ideal situation.

Also, you may have noticed that I decided my girls' lesson order as we arrived at Ms. J's home. By making such decisions (small in my eyes, and big in my children's) on the fly, I created unnecessary tension between my children and me. After a year of doing lessons every Tuesday, we could have easily established a fair method to decide who would go first. Due to my inconsistency in managing who would go first each time, I undermined my influence as a teacher and guide to my children. Someone needed to decide the lesson order, but by being arbitrary about the decision, I limited my later influence with other children.

Workbook Questions:

- What kind of conflicts can I anticipate between my children?

- What could I do to prepare for and prevent possible conflicts between my children?

C–Choose to Be Proactive

Prioritize Socio-Emotional Skills Development, Not Just Academic, Musical, and Athletic Skills

Despite the recent emphasis in Western society on developing emotional intelligence (EQ), which is the ability to identify and manage your own *emotions* and the *emotions* of others, most parents spend much more time providing for the academic, musical, and athletic training for children than ensuring that they acquire better social skills. As my overscheduling and impatient responses to my children's different outbursts show, I acted as if I valued certain skills, such as violin or piano playing, over developing and teaching conflict management and communication skills.

Parents want children to learn to be happy, cooperative members of society, but we do not afford as much time, value, or emphasis on teaching critical communication skills, which demand greater attention from parents. Parents assume that children will learn important social skills somehow, outside our presence, despite the dramatic need we find in the adult world for communication experts, lawyers, therapists, counselors, judges, and the like.

Rather than assume children will independently pick up the necessary socio-emotional skills needed to manage conflict in their lives, we need to teach communication skills directly when appropriate circumstances surface in daily life. Our framing of such conflict crises as learning opportunities, rather than deliberate efforts by children to sabotage our well-laid plans, may provide the momentum we need to reevaluate our priorities in teaching life skills as life unfolds.

In my case, I focused and put greater value on Ben's completing his piano worksheet in time for his lesson that night, rather than spending time with Jack to help him work through his frustration over losing the foosball game to Ben. I also valued Ms. J's and her children's peace and harmony over mine and my children's peace, stability, and learning. Although, I didn't need to work out all our problems in Ms. J's basement in that moment, I did need to appreciate and respond to the raw skills gap these specific conflict situations exposed in our family life.

In my impatience, I demanded that Jack be quiet, even when the situation begged for my guidance to teach him how to respond to frustration, competition, and sibling rivalry. Rather than dismiss and forget what occurred on either of those Tuesdays, I could have later evaluated how to teach Jack and his siblings to manage their angry feelings during competitive or isolating situations. Now I know that I can teach them how to express their personal feelings constructively, using rich vocabulary, rather than just telling them to stop screaming or crying.

Since those events, I now stay aware of my children's communication skills gaps and try to teach those needed skills with a long-term perspective in mind. Just as Jack hasn't learned to play soccer in one afternoon, likely, he will need many days of learning how to express frustration in appropriate ways before he responds skillfully in a random or new conflict situation.

Workbook Questions:

- What skills do each of my children currently lack in terms of conflict management or communication skills?

- When do I notice the need for these skills among my children?

- How could I help my children gain these needed skills?

H–Help Kids as Needed

Assume Kids Will Need Help at First, but Gradually Withdraw Your Assistance

Despite parents' view that they are "always" intervening in children's conflicts, research confirms that about half the time parents don't get involved at all. One study in 1999 by child development researchers Dr. Laurie F. Kramer, the late Lisa A. Perozynski, and Tsai-Yen Chun reported that parents ignore their young children's conflicts 45 percent of the time for mothers and 56 percent of the time for fathers. A related study in 1997 by Dr. Michal Perlman and Dr. Hildy Ross reported that parents do not intervene 43 percent of the time when their children fight. While mothers tend to be proactive slightly more often than fathers, both parents are three times more likely to ignore their children's conflicts than step in. Clearly, parents perceive their interventions, but may not realize how often they do not help children through their conflicts, even when they need support and guidance.

Given that Ben and Amy are still young, ages seven and five, respectively, I not only needed to supervise their care, but also needed (and still need) to teach them how to manage their emotions and interactions with each other. In short, they required more parent intervention than I chose to offer at Ms. J's house on the first Tuesday.

Although I chose to punish Amy and Ben together, I could have first calmed their feelings (without punishing) then helped develop a sustainable plan for us all. I missed these steps first by trying to ignore their demands for attention and then by moving toward punishment and immediate reconciliation (which failed despite my threats and demands). Amy's and Ben's outbursts represented a lack of skills and development rather than a deliberate attack on my peace and well-being. I was impressed with myself that I could sit on Mrs. J's couch calmly while my children screamed, but needed a better plan than just waiting out their screaming.

Research by Dr. Afshan Siddiqui and Dr. Hildy Ross of the University of Waterloo confirms that when we leave our children to their own problem-solving devices following a conflict, both younger and older siblings experience increased conflict and hostility with each other. In addition, unresolved conflict predicts greater conflict in the future. Even when children are able to resolve conflicts with each other, an older or otherwise more powerful child will usually "win" or dominate the conflict resolution process. Research places bets on both children "losing" in sibling conflict situations that parents ignore. Ben, as the older sibling in the conflict, had only a slightly higher chance to come out on top because of his increased age, size, and language skills compared to Amy, his younger sister.

My youngest children, Ben and Amy, needed greater support to work through their issues. Also, given Jack's unfamiliarity with both the violin teacher's home environment, the foosball game, and his tendency toward avoiding confrontation until he explodes, I needed to scaffold his conflict management learning without judging and punishing him, even though he was the older sibling in the conflict. Shaming Jack into proper behavior only exposed developmental gaps that distanced us from the effective problem-solving approaches we needed to prevent similar future conflicts. Instead of a judge, Jack needed a calm guide and teacher.

In both cases, I behaved as judge and punisher rather than as an advocate or guide to working through issues originally belonging to my children. As I caught "fire" with conflict, I created further conflict situations both in and outside my family. My experiences with Jack and Ben illustrated the tendency most parents have to quickly assign blame to one child when entering children's conflicts with each other.

Parental Tendency Toward Blaming One Child

As discussed in the previous chapter, researchers have discovered that when parents assume the guilt of one child over the other in a conflict setting, parents tend to use much less collaborative conflict resolution methods with their children and are more likely to intervene as judges with rewards and punishments.

In first tending to Ben and Amy as they fought with each other, I assumed bilateral blame, so I took both children into my arms and let them cry it out, punishing both with the loss of computer privileges. I did not determine who was to blame, nor did I care at that point. Assuming a competitive approach, I demanded quiet from my children and only received greater screaming and anger.

In my interactions with Jack, I focused entirely on his outburst, assuming only he needed to change his behavior. I barely asked Ben questions about the conflict. Instead, I focused on getting Jack to be quiet. In my search for speedy reconciliation and avoidance of an embarrassing (to me) situation, I targeted Jack and moved forward with my method of asserting parent authority.

As also discussed in the previous chapter, research confirms that once parents have determined a particular conflict management strategy, such as control methods (with threats or demands) or child-centered methods of collaboration (with questions or a discussion of feelings), parents continue to use the same approach as the conflict continues or extends into the future. In short, the initial conflict management choice tends to predict later methods of choice.

Upon reflection, I realized that I had unconsciously followed these common parenting tendencies to assume blame and punish my children accordingly. However, now that I realize my own tendency toward assigning blame up front, I actively work against this bias and withhold blame before I've discussed an issue of sibling conflict. As I consciously gravitate toward the role of teacher and guide rather than judge, I position myself to help my children resolve their own problems rather than upsetting the balance between my child's need for autonomy and my desire for reconciliation.

Workbook Questions:

- When do my kids need my help to work out their conflicts with each other?

- In which areas could I gradually withdraw my intervention to allow for more child autonomy in problem-solving?

- Do I tend to blame one child when sibling conflict erupts?

- How can I improve my approach to intervening and avoid blaming my children for their conflicts?

M—Mediate

To Mediate or Not

Parents may use a combination of the five conflict approaches to resolve the types of conflicts my children and I experienced on Tuesdays. But, I entirely neglected collaborative methods, like mediation, that include helping my children talk through, empathize, and brainstorm with each other to solve joint problems. In research settings, parent-led mediation produces many positive outcomes for parents and children:

Mediation Benefits:

- More easily share their perspectives
- Increased listening
- More explanation of personal actions
- Sincerer apologizing
- More suggesting of solutions
- Better clarification of unresolved issues
- More even balance of power
- More acceptance of developed plans
- More requests to create joint plans
- More likely to begin resolution process
- Solutions more constructive than those developed by parents
- Less blaming by older sibling
- More balanced sharing by siblings

- Younger siblings empowered to share more ideas
- Parents more likely to discuss emotions
- Children more likely to discuss emotions
- Parents reported being calmer during resolution
- Increased parent and child satisfaction with the process
- More constructive outcomes
- Greater compromise

These results, which families can expect from parent-led mediation, suggest that children collaborate more effectively with each other when parents provide support for a constructive conflict resolution process with their children, like mediation.

As a parent-mediator, rather than making most of the important decisions for my fighting children, I could have guided them in making their own decisions with each other. I had several opportunities for using mediation between my children to settle the following questions:

- Who goes first on the violin each week? (Amy and Emma)
- What kind of arrangement would work for the kids to provide supervision and activities during the lessons? (Emma, Jack, Ben, and Amy)
- What happens if children disrupt violin lessons? (Amy, Ben, Mom, and maybe the violin teacher)

- What are the rules for playing foosball, and what happens if an "accidental" goal is scored? (Jack and Ben)

In the next chapter, I focus on parent-led mediation and how it represents a model for joint problem-solving that allows parents to actively participate in resolving their children's conflicts. As teachers and guides rather than judges in resolving conflict, parents reserve decision-making power for the children in conflict. In parent-led mediation, children practice the skills of sharing perspectives, asking clarifying questions, seeing the conflict from another person's perspective, reframing the conflict as joint problems, and working out solutions both children can accept.

Sometimes parents miss significant opportunities to teach these critical life skills that involve collaboration with others because of the quest to preserve peace, reconcile quickly, and keep to a schedule. And certainly, we won't get collaboration right every time. But as we deliberately embrace the learning situations we encounter, we enable children to grow from, rather than learn to avoid, the conflicts that everyone encounters in daily life.

Avoid Expecting Perfection in Social Development

At first, I was drawn into Amy and Ben's conflict with each other because they distracted the ongoing violin lesson. While I did not become angry in that situation, Ben and Amy made such a fuss that Ms. J began to develop hostile feelings toward us, as did her children, who could not concentrate on their homework. The following week, as Jack began fighting with Ben, I responded to my boys' conflict in an intense and embarrassed way because I was worried about the past conflict with Ms. J. My desire to protect my ego prevented me from providing the necessary teaching my children needed in that situation.

In my encounter with Jack, I recognize that my own pride prevented a real opportunity to listen and teach my son about getting along with his brother in a competitive situation. Ultimately, I want Jack to learn how to have a great relationship with all his siblings, but for the immediate gratification of my ego, I would not have demanded submission to my will. Then my son and I perceived incompatible goals, conflict behavior, and hostility, which characterize the experience of conflict.

Workbook Questions:

- What types of sibling conflicts in my home would benefit from using parent-led mediation?
- When do I expect too much of my children in managing conflict?
- How can I help support my children in their efforts to collaborate to solve problems?

E—Enjoy the Process

We Get to Know Each Other and Can Strengthen Relationships Through Conflict

As I mentioned, I dreaded Tuesdays for a variety of reasons, especially because of the many conflicts we experienced. But, the conflicts helped me realize that I needed to make several changes in our family life, including modifying our schedule, reviewing our family priorities, and discussing my children's preferences and needs related to my expectations and abilities as a parent. In short, by treating our conflicts as learning experiences, we have discovered better ways to focus our time and effort as a family. Through our conflict experiences, we discovered many unmet needs and have adjusted our priorities to create greater harmony and purpose in our daily lives, especially on Tuesdays.

I hope to become more conscious and proactive in my parenting, despite my family's imperfect communication skills. As I mentioned before, when my young children made mistakes with learning to talk, walk, or ride a bike, I did not criticize or ignore their failures or efforts. Instead, I jumped to encourage improvement and greater effort so they wouldn't get discouraged when they did not perform perfectly.

Likewise, through experiences like our dreaded Tuesdays, I became more aware of my own limitations and need to improve how I manage conflict. It reminded me of the way sibling conflict can transform and spread into parent-child or spousal conflict. My conflict resolution skills need to grow alongside my children's as we deliberately practice more constructive communication patterns.

As I understand my own conflict tendencies, refine my personal communication habits, and reframe conflict learning in terms of other typical patterns for child development, my ability to assist my children improves. The oft-repeated request in airplane flights for parents to secure their own oxygen masks before assisting their children rings true with conflict resolution too. As we get a grip on our own expectations and tendencies, we strengthen the capacity to become guides, teachers, and examples to encourage children's positive management of conflict in their daily lives. The TEACH ME acronym serves to prepare us to be the kind of parents our kids need so they can learn positive approaches to conflict management.

Workbook Questions:

- How can I change my attitude toward my children's ongoing learning about conflict management?

- What can I do to support my children in revisiting conflict solutions that have not or are not currently working in our home?

In the next chapter, I explore a specific collaborative framework for encouraging positive sibling conflict management: parent-led mediation. I share the research behind it and the potential benefits of its use in the home. While parent-led mediation represents only one tool in our collaborative approach to conflict, research demonstrates the power of parent-led mediation to increase child autonomy while facilitating reconciliation and peace. Through the process of parent-led mediation, we guide our children not only to learn critical problem-solving skills, but also to develop empathy and perspective-taking skills, which support all positive human interaction as children grow into adolescence and adulthood.

Chapter 7 Summary

The TEACH ME method focuses on preparing parents to teach their children constructive conflict management principles and strategies.

Test Expectations
Establish Patterns
Anticipate Conflict
Choose to be Proactive
Help Kids as Needed
Mediate
Enjoy the Process

CHAPTER 8

INTRODUCTION TO PARENT-LED MEDIATION:

BECOMING A PARENT-MEDIATOR

Mediation in Paradise

A few years ago, during a beautiful day on the British Virgin Island of Saint Kitts, my four-year-old daughter, Amy, and I were enjoying a lovely explanation about tropical plants, such as the wild cashew, hibiscus, and aloe vera. Our small tour group of ten people stood huddled around our guide on the side of a winding highway road overlooking the Caribbean Sea. Suddenly, a male voice hurled expletives through the air, "f'this, f'that." I looked to find a native taxi driver yelling at what appeared to be an elderly European couple seated one behind the other in a closed white minivan with open windows.

Our unflappable guide, Roosevelt, chose to ignore the

shouting and continued his discussion of wild cashews with our small crowd of American tourists. The shouting continued, the taxi driver becoming louder and more menacing.

Although I was still a student, because of my training as a certified mediator, I turned anxiously to a female member of my tour group and asked, "Should we do something about this? I am a trained mediator." She didn't respond; in fact, no one attempted to get involved to assuage the taxi driver's rage or protect the elderly couple from his wrath.

After realizing that no one else would intervene, I decided to approach the angry man and attempt to help resolve this very public dispute. I felt a sense of social obligation to protect the elderly couple, so I walked toward the raging man standing by the shiny, white minivan.

The taxi driver didn't strike me, so I pressed on and asked, "What is bothering you?"

While pointing an accusatory finger at a long-legged elderly man in holiday shorts whom I could see clearly through the open windows, he shouted, "He will not wait for me to open the van door. He keeps pushing and pushing on the handle. He does not f'ing listen."

Reflecting back to him what I'd heard, I said, "It sounds like you're concerned about the man using the door handle. Is that true?"

Still raging, the taxi driver said, "Yes. He will not listen; he just keeps pushing and pushing on the handle when I asked him to stop."

I turned to the elderly couple and asked if they were

okay, if they felt safe. They looked back at me and said, "We just want to get out of the car."

Then, I asked the elderly pair, "What were you doing with the handle?"

With a heavy German accent, the man replied, "I just wanted to get out of the car to visit the shop; then this man started yelling at me and will not stop."

I wondered why the taxi driver did not want his passenger to get out of the van to visit the roadside shop of fruits and trinkets. I asked, "Why don't you want him to use the handle?"

Clearly frustrated but willing to respond to my question, the driver said, "He's going to break it. This is my new car."

"Oh," I said, "you're worried about him breaking your new car by pushing on the handle?"

As I restated his sentiment, he became noticeably more focused. As he pointed to the minivan, he said, "This is my new car, and just last week some guests broke this part"—pointing to another area inside the car—"and they didn't even pay for it. They have no respect for us and do not care about me."

At this point, I understood his deep frustration and anger and reflected this back to him. "So, someone recently broke your car that you just bought. It sounds like you're worried that this man is going to break the handle and ruin your car too. Do I have that right?"

"Yes," he replied more quietly. It was clear he was feeling calmer. Continuing in this vein, he said, "If I have a broken car, no one will drive with me; then I will not be able to earn any money. This is my brand new car."

Turning to the couple, I asked if they would let the taxi driver open the door for them so the door would not get broken.

The couple replied, nearly in sync, "Yes. We just want to continue with the tour. Let's go." Forgetting the adjacent trinket shop, they seemed to want to drive on away from this episode.

"Are you okay now to continue the tour?" I asked the taxi driver.

Calmly, but firmly, he said, "Yes," and got back into the driver's seat.

As they pulled back onto the highway along the blue ocean, I marveled that the mediation techniques had worked.

Even with strangers, one of whom was particularly upset, who were from three different countries and diverse backgrounds, we could find peace among ourselves.

Within our families, given that we have similar backgrounds, how much more successful could we be in applying these principles at home? At this pivotal moment in my life, I realized that, to raise a mediator, I must become a mediator, or someone willing to use a collaborative approach to resolve conflicts, regardless of the potentially high emotions of the parties.

Understanding Collaboration Then Teaching Collaboration

Once parents understand their natural conflict tendencies and the skills needed for the five conflict management approaches (avoiding, compromising, accommodating, competing, and collaborating), they learn that different situations require different approaches. It helps to possess a wide range of skills for different conflict needs and situations.

Knowing that parents have natural tendencies to either ignore sibling conflict or intervene too heavily as judges or punishers, we have some work to do before we approach children with the idea of mediating. Perhaps, like us, they will collaborate and teach collaboration if they know how and if we make collaborative processes, like mediation, a family practice.

In my own life, despite my love of peaceful interactions, I had never imagined myself as a mediator, especially with my children. But, in recognizing my natural (and learned) desire to avoid or intrude too much in settling my children's conflicts, I consciously decided to learn how to collaborate and effectively teach mediation to my kids. These are two different skill sets: modeling or living collaborative practices and teaching them. These two skills intertwine to make for a successful parent-mediator.

In this chapter, I explore how to become a parent-mediator and teach mediation skills to children following the steps in the TEACH ME acronym. In the chapter that follows, I apply these skills and insights in several different conflict situations, some suitable for mediation and others that require a different approach. In the last chapter of the book, I share practices that support and solidify parent-led mediation in the home, such as building parent communication skills, holding regular family meetings, establishing and upholding family rules, and practicing clear, compassionate communication.

The Tussle over a Blanket and the Coveted Spot on the Couch

In our living room, there is a heavenly, cozy spot on the couch near a window that looks onto the grassy lawn of our neighborhood park. Besides the view, I had bought a super soft blue blanket that made this corner of the couch a nice snuggle. The kids discovered the comfort of this spot, which they all preferred, especially on cold winter mornings before the heater turned on.

Early on, I helped Emma and Ben negotiate who would get to sit in the spot during specific times before school. One morning, after Emma had left, my five-year-old kindergartner, Amy, and my seven-year-old, Ben, fought over who would sit in the coveted cozy spot with the blue blanket.

As they were fighting, I was tempted to issue an edict: either they could share the blanket while sitting side by side or take ten minutes one after the other in the spot. Though this was an attractive solution, I resisted, knowing that I had pledged to stop interfering in every conflict as a judge. With a few minutes to spare before breakfast, this time, I attempted to mediate by asking: "Ben, what would you like?"

As expected, Ben stated, with a resolute look, "I want the blanket and the spot. I was here first."

Next, I turned to Amy who was thrashing on the floor and grabbing for the blanket under dispute. I asked her, "What would you like?"

Again, as I expected, Amy whined. "I want the blanket and to sit in that spot. Ben always gets that spot. It's not fair."

She was defiant, whiney, and bordering on pure emotion (suggesting to me that a regular drama scene was about to unfold). I had just woken up and didn't feel like dealing with my kids' fighting, but I pursued resolving the situation at hand.

At this point, both Ben and Amy had each given me information I already knew, and that they already knew about each other. I wondered if this attempt at mediation was going to work.

I moved forward with my chosen strategy. "It sounds like you both want the same thing at the same time. Is that right?"

They both agreed, but then they began campaigning loudly for their rights to the coveted spot. Somewhat bewildered by my belabored process of asking so many questions, Ben and Amy's eyes seemed to ask, "What are you doing, Mom?"

Feeling frustrated and eager to prepare breakfast, I almost dictated the same compromise I had thought of initially, but, again, I resisted for the sake of practicing what I preached about mediation. I took a breath (to keep my patience), then asked them, "What can we do to make it fair for both of you? Can you think of anything that would work?"

They appeared to be disinterested in this unusual process of talking about this conflict. But suddenly, Ben suggested that they use the blanket to make a tent on the other side of the room. Amy immediately agreed, and they began making their blanket tent right before my eyes on the nearby bench.

The idea of making a tent had never crossed my mind as

a solution to their problem. But, the minute Ben suggested it, Amy quickly agreed and the conflict dissipated, resulting in dual cooperation to construct the tent with the former object of contention. They had different needs and desires from what I had anticipated for them; my compromise solution would never have addressed the possibility of tent-making.

On another day, perhaps in the near future, we may come back to this conflict, but for now, the three of us have a small experience with mediation to lean on. The next time Amy and Ben fight about the spot on the couch, I can remind them of how they resolved their past differences with their own creative idea. In short, I will remind them of their own previous self-reliance that worked! Yes, I assisted in the process, but only in helping them to arrive at and implement their own ideas.

While this is a seemingly trite issue in our household, this experience helped me to build my children's confidence in conflict resolution and served as practice of critical listening and brainstorming skills—for the kids *and* me. I imagine that the issues my children fight over will become increasingly complex as they mature, but we can start with small, everyday conflicts that fail to disappear with avoiding or accommodating. Also, as I consciously turn from judge or punisher to mediator, I create an environment for new types of interactions between my children that involve empathy, problem solving, and perspective taking.

Overview of Mediation

Perhaps, you have never met a mediator and never imagined yourself as one. Or, if you have met with a professional mediator before, it may have been a brief encounter to resolve a difficult problem, like child custody or a neighborhood dispute. Few parents have been formally trained in mediation processes and skills that build on sound communication practices like listening, restating, clarifying, reframing, and summarizing our perspectives, interests, and problems. But, these fundamental mediation or communication skills are not beyond the reach of ordinary people.

The Role of Mediator

Mediators serve as a third-party communication assistant to two or more parties with a conflict. Rather than judging or evaluating the worth or value of a conflict and its possible resolutions, a mediator seeks to facilitate communication so that parties in conflict can not only understand each other, but also possibly reconcile their differences. To unleash collaborative processes, mediators strive to reframe conflict in terms of joint interests so that the conflict parties focus on problem-solving based on ideas and interests rather than solely on people's past wrongdoings and their related hostile feelings.

Oftentimes, mediation does not help resolve all issues. Even then, it provides a forum where people can establish ground rules for communication, share feelings and perspectives, clarify issues, reframe conflicts into joint problems, and brainstorm solutions.

Mediation Addresses the Three P's of Conflict

Generally, mediation addresses the three elements of all conflicts—people, process, and problem—in a balanced way so that parties feel equal in power and the ability to participate in resolving a specific conflict.

More specifically, the mediation process addresses these elements in the following ways:

- **People**: In mediation, each person has an opportunity to share his or her thoughts, feelings, and perspectives without interruption. They may ask clarifying questions to understand thought processes, background, and other important relationship qualities that influence the conflict resolution process and potential solutions.

- **Process:** Through a structured seven-step process assisted by a mediator, each person gets a fair hearing of their goals and interest. The process ensures that each party gets time to share their side of the story without interruption or accusations. In addition, the mediator manages the steps so that each is followed in a specific order to offer a greater chance for success. In reframing, the mediator turns hostile feelings about people and things into energy for resolving jointly-held issues.

- **Problem**: Each party has an opportunity to present their understanding of the problem independently, along with their emotions and experiences in the conflict. While each side gets a turn to share their perspective, the mediator attempts to reframe independent interpretations into a cohesive, jointly-held problem. With a reframed collective problem, the mediator tries to help the parties focus on satisfying both of their interests through a future-based solution, rather than dwelling on negative emotions and past experiences.

Minimal Training for Parent-Led Mediation

While mediation may sound as if it requires years of study and apprenticeship, to become a parent-mediator, parents need much less training. With only an average of ninety minutes of formal mediation training, mothers and fathers in controlled research studies managed to learn and apply mediation principles effectively in their own homes with their preschoolers to twelve- year-old children. Your most important contributions to learning parent-led mediation are a willing mind and some patience as you and your children build new skills and habits with each other.

What Roles Do We Each Play in Mediation?

In parent-led mediation, parents step out of the role of problem-solving judge to become a communications assistant. As a parent-mediator, we support our children talking through issues, hearing both sides, brainstorming possible solutions, deciding to resolve the conflict, and reality testing that decision. Rather than determine the outcome, parent-mediators guide children toward crafting their own solutions to resolve their differences with each other. We serve to control the communication process of mediation (i.e., uphold rules, balance the conversation) while children control the decision or outcome of the process.

Facilitating as a Mediator

Although it's unlikely we will ever be or feel completely neutral in these disputes—this may be next to impossible as a parent—we can learn to refrain from judging or evaluating the validity of our children's expressed thoughts, feelings, and ideas while participating in the mediation process. Parents can supplement and guide the communication process as needed with children who struggle to verbalize thoughts and ideas. And despite providing this type of help, we can learn to facilitate rather than directly assert our thoughts, ideas, and opinions into our children's mediation experiences with each other.

Strong Support Followed by Gradual Withdrawal of Parent Participation

At first, parents must provide a lot of guidance to children and reinforcement of the mediation process with its basic rules and steps. Gradually, as children gain familiarity with the mediation process, enjoy more balanced power with their siblings, and strengthen the communication skills required for success, parents can withdraw elements of participation. Research by Dr. Avigail Ram and Dr. Hildy Ross of the University of Waterloo confirms that as children mature cognitively, develop more abstract thinking, and increase their reasoning skills and vocabulary, they generally require less assistance by parents in crafting solutions to conflicts with their siblings. Of course, exceptions exist, so parents might always serve as backup for children who are working out conflicts with each other.

What Are the Steps to Parent-Led Mediation?

Using the acronym from the last chapter, TEACH ME, I outline the specific steps for parent-led mediation. With each TEACH ME step, I outline significant points from parent-led mediation research and related conflict studies to support the discussion. Step by step, parents can prepare themselves to identify appropriate situations and communication skills to develop over time—certainly not overnight.

Parent-led mediation is not a perfect solution or panacea to all parenting woes regarding sibling conflict. However, recent parent-led mediation research reveals powerful, positive results for children and entire families, even over time. You have everything you need to learn the basic steps to successful parent-led mediation based on sound communication skills and principles used in facilitative negotiation.

With the TEACH ME structure, we follow these seven basic steps or phases for successful parent-led mediation:

Time to Assess

Establish Structure

Acknowledge Alternate Views

Clarify Emotions and Interests

Hear All Ideas and Reframe Conflict

Make Joint Decisions

Expect Changes

T—Time to Assess

Overview

Mediation requires time. Regardless of a parent's ultimate choice of conflict management approach, they need to take the time to assess a conflict situation to see if mediation is suitable. If we choose mediation, we must understand that the process takes more time than other common approaches to resolving sibling conflict. But, even if we don't have the time to resolve the conflict this way when it first erupts, we could consider mediating the conflict when time and circumstance allow.

Beyond time constraints, parents should consider conflict intensity, how often the same type of conflict reoccurs, and children's communication skills and abilities when they decide whether to mediate a sibling conflict. I use a few guidelines and questions to help me determine whether parent-led mediation would be effective or appropriate in a particular situation.

Conflict Intensity—How Intense Is This Conflict between My Children?

Most sibling conflicts are short-lived, about forty-five seconds on average for conflicts that develop between pre-schoolers. Many conflicts grow in frequency and intensity if not resolved in the early stages before emotions flare out of control and children's positions harden into true hostility. Parents do tend to interfere in their children's more intense conflicts. But, knowing that conflicts escalate if not resolved, perhaps we might treat smaller conflicts with greater care. In short, we can choose to treat mole hills of conflict before they emerge as mountains of hostility and inflexibility.

We've all experienced the way conflicts can escalate from lack of resolution as well as the absence of adequate structured opportunities to voice natural frustration. Like adults, children need secure ways to express their very real emotions and make requests that reflect their needs and desires. Although children's needs and desires may differ from our own in complexity, the fundamental need to be heard, understood, and respected remain the same regardless of age.

When considering children's conflicts, you may ask yourself if the conflict is intense or important enough to warrant mediation. To guide you further in deciding whether to mediate, it helps to consider conflict reoccurrence to understand how important this issue is to children in conflict and the family as a whole.

Conflict Reoccurrence–How Often Are My Children Fighting about This Same Issue?

Parents can ask themselves two fundamental questions about conflict reoccurrence to judge the importance of a specific conflict to contending children.

(1) Does this conflict represent a major ongoing issue that keeps reoccurring without any successful resolution?

(2) Has this issue failed to go away using other more common approaches, such as compromise, avoidance, or a parent making a decision for the children?

As we reflect on how often certain conflicts reoccur in our households, we become more aware of certain topics and patterns that fuel children's contentions with each other. In addition, as we study the intensity and reoccurrence of particular conflicts, we can more consciously select conflict management approaches that suit the situation and that may be more effective than our current strategies to create harmony in our homes. Remember the parent tendency to keep using the same conflict management strategy as a conflict continues.

To understand how to approach various types of conflicts based on intensity, reoccurrence, and importance to the parties, conflict theorists Dr. Kenneth W. Thomas and Dr. Ralph H. Kilmann developed a set of basic questions to ask when involved in a personal conflict. Below, I include a modified list of six questions to further guide you in choosing when to intervene with parent-led mediation. The answers in parentheses weigh in favor of parent-led mediation.

1. Is the conflict simple or complex? (More complex.)

2. How important is the topic to both children? (Important to one or more parties.)

3. Is there enough time to address the conflict? (Ample time or at least some flexibility.)

4. Is there enough trust between the parties to allow them to share their true needs and concerns with one

another? (Trust either necessary or desired.)

5. Do the children have good listening and communication skills? (Developed or at least supported by a parent-led mediator.)

6. How important is the relationship to both people? Do they want the relationship to last? (Although siblings may refute the importance of their relationship, parents know that it is important and needs to be nurtured through parental guidance.)

Typically, close family relationships represent an ideal type of relationship for both learning and applying collaborative conflict-resolution practices like parent-led mediation. Of course, plenty of limited, more mundane conflicts between siblings do not require mediation. When you consider social learning for a lifetime, the home setting provides one of the best places to learn how to collaborate from a very early age— perhaps much earlier than most people would assume despite young children's tantrums and limited verbal expression.

Children's Current Communication Skills and Abilities

When Are My Children Ready to Learn How to Mediate?

Young children are able to imitate many sophisticated communication skills involved with mediation even before they are able to reason in abstract ways. Research suggests that children as early as age three can participate in mediation in a meaningful way. Parents can teach them while they are young and before they develop habits that need to be relearned or modified later in life. As children mature, they will be equipped with specialized communications skills to deal with more complex conflicts that call for a more thoughtful process and sophisticated communication styles than mere win-lose behaviors associated with avoiding or competing.

As I mention in earlier chapters, children, especially young children, learn best through modeling and direct teaching of communication and interpersonal skills. When we use these methods in our homes, we openly encourage children to develop critical problem-solving, empathy, and perspective-taking skills that are not emphasized in our prevailing culture. In parent-led mediation, we help children discuss their emotions, their personal interests, and how they think about the problems. We provide a safe environment where learning is encouraged, rather than criticized, and we don't expect their conflict management skills to be perfect. In sum, we deliberately coach our kids to be effective communicators.

What Should I Expect When Mediating with Preschoolers?

Preschoolers, especially on the younger end, will have more limited vocabularies, smaller attention spans, and less emotional regulation, so we need to shorten the time we spend to talk things out. However, we can build communication skills outside of conflict situations. For example, in situations that don't involve conflict, children can practice saying what they need, reflecting what we say to them, and creating clarifying questions to better understand another person's point of view. As the model or teacher, we need to help children learn to calm their emotions when they get upset. We might suggest taking a few minutes to play with toys, have a snack, or run around outside before we attempt to talk with them about a problem.

A Caution Concerning the Tendency to Treat Our Children's Skills Interchangeably

Different children behave differently during sibling conflict, and this may vary according to their age, sex, personality, education, and temperament. Along those lines, we cannot assume that each child will have the same ability to master these skills or stay calm while discussing conflict. For example, an older child could have more difficulty listening or explaining his feelings than the younger child. Although it's reasonable to expect greater maturity from older children, we need to adjust our expectations with each child and take them as they are and what they're capable of in the moment.

The following sections are filled with exercises. These will take time and energy to complete, but are well worth the effort.

E–Establish Structure

After you determine that mediation is the best approach and everyone is calm enough to proceed, you will need to provide a structure for the mediation process, especially during the first several attempts. Children need help to determine an appropriate time and place for a discussion that may last for more than a few minutes. We can adapt the mediation process to situations away from the home, but we need to ensure that we have ample time; a suitable and quiet setting for sharing of thoughts, perspectives, and feelings; and no interruptions, which could possibly escalate a conflict situation.

Just as in the early days of teaching children to ride a bike or play an instrument, we'll need to guide children ever so closely in mediation depending upon their skill level, personality, and temperament. Regardless of their differences, as parent-mediators, we start by introducing, training, and initiating children into the process of parent-led mediation.

First, given power imbalances between older and younger children and the potentially volatile feelings fueled by the conflict, parents need to lay out the structure for and guide the mediation process. Remember these basic mediation steps include the following:

Time to Assess
Establish Structure
Acknowledge Alternate Views
Clarify Emotions and Interests
Hear All Ideas and Reframe Conflict
Make Joint Decisions
Expect Changes

When you apply these seven steps, you can modify the length and depth according to the intensity of the conflict and your children's attention spans. Although we want to avoid controlling mediation outcomes or decisions, providing a structure for and steering the mediation process is important so that each child feels confident they will get a fair hearing and the opportunity to offer their own tailored solutions to the problems they share.

Roles and Process

For starters, you may need to explain all the mediation steps to children, but not always. Remember in my mediation of the blanket tug-of-war, I casually used the steps without a sit-down interaction or explanation of the process. Though your explanation might be as simple as "let's talk through or mediate the conflict," be sure to clarify the roles you each play: you help the kids talk through their conflict, and they come up with the solutions to their problems. In short, we may briefly describe the roles each of us will play in solving the problem. You don't need to call it a mediation because a technical term may be distracting and unnecessary, especially for young children with more limited verbal expression and less emotional regulation.

Rules

After describing the process and roles, focus on developing a short list of basic ground rules for talking. If your children have trouble coming up with basic rules, you can provide a general template for their communication problem-solving, such as the following:

- No interrupting
- No name-calling
- No accusations
- Focus on talking about the future and what you need, not what happened in the past

You'll have much greater buy-in if your kids help draft the initial set of rules. Even simply asking for the kids' okay on the rules we suggest may be enough for commitment to the rules during the interaction. Throughout the process, you may still need to remind them of the rules even after they agree to follow them.

Finally, it's important to model respectful behavior and allow your children to express their emotions in constructive ways. You want your children to avoid name-calling, accusations, and threats, but they need to feel they can openly express how they feel and what they need. You help them find the balance by providing space for each child to share their side of the story and vent their emotions, then focus on the future and potential solutions that will address everyone's needs.

A—Acknowledge Alternate Views

The purpose of this step is to allow each child to share their perspective without interruption, accusation, or blaming and then listen to another person's perspective without interruption, accusation, or blaming. During the opening sharing time, and what is likely the most volatile time during the mediation, allow each child to express his or her side of the story openly. Such open sharing may include venting of strong emotions. While we may strongly dislike listening to others vent strong emotions, if we want to resolve a conflict, we need to include the option for sharing of strong emotions. As part of the deliberate conflict management process, we allow for the undiscussables to surface and be addressed through a constructive framework.

Children may not easily acknowledge their siblings' views of the conflict, but even very young children can learn to see others' perspectives over time with guidance and rein-forcement of the rules and process. You pave the way by creating a fair process with respect for everyone's thoughts and feelings, especially those that might seem off-limits in other circumstances.

To ensure a safe process for true sharing of feelings, ask yourself and your children the following questions:

- Do I get to say something without you getting mad at me?

- Will you hear me out until I'm done sharing?

- Do I avoid accusing or threatening my siblings when they disagree with me?

- Do I avoid judging what the other person says?

- Where and when can I get out all that I would like to say?

- Will I be punished if I say what I really think and feel?

EXERCISES FOR PARENTS

Exercise 1: Listen without Interruption with Adults

With or without explaining what you're doing, listen to your spouse, partner, or close friend vent. Refrain from making any judgments about what you hear. Paraphrase, empathize, and ask good questions to clarify what the person has shared. See if you can uncover the real interests of the person who has shared with you.

Exercise 2: Listen and Provide Affirmation to Your Child

When your child becomes upset about something, hear them out before making a judgment or trying to solve their immediate problem. Take the time to rephrase what you heard from your child so that he or she feels understood. For example, you can say things like "It sounds like you're really frustrated" or "You seem like you really got hurt" or "It sounds like you were really scared." Follow those affirmations with clarifying questions like, "Could you tell me more about it?" or "What made you so mad?"

Social Learning and Understanding Multiple Interpretations of an Ambiguous Conflict

Many children who are younger than seven or eight lack the ability to understand the possibility for multiple interpretations of an ambiguous conflict situation. But, through research in 2007 by Dr. Hildy Ross and Julie Smith of the University of Waterloo, even preschoolers demonstrated that they could understand multiple explanations for ambiguous conflict. Ross and Smith's research suggests that through modeling and direct teaching by parents, young children can learn to imitate and incorporate much more sophisticated social skills than children without similar experiences.

In addition, in a 1997 study, Drs. Judy Dunn and Carla Herrera discovered one long-term benefit of learning to listen to others' viewpoints. Their research revealed that when mothers use other-focused reasoning, children benefit by developing more constructive management with friends and other peers. On the flip side, when mothers use self-focused reasoning, children tend to replicate the opposite pattern (i.e., destructive relationship management). This means that children who are taught by their mothers to consider others' perspectives in a conflict tend to imitate this constructive behavior in their social interactions in many other settings.

Perspective taking and empathy are key positive skills that come out of the mediation process; these skills influence relationships throughout childhood, adolescence, and adulthood. Because children's skill levels will vary, you'll need to provide very direct and specific guidance to help them learn how to share without blaming or accusing and listen without interrupting. We do this by reinforcing the ground rules and modeling positive examples of the behavior we expect.

Example of Asking and Allowing for Alternate Views as a Parent-Mediator

My first step is to reassure my children of a fair process and equal time to vent their feelings and share their perspectives. I begin by telling them the following:

"We're going to spend a few minutes talking about what happened. You'll each have a turn to share your side of the story while the other two of us listen without interrupting. Jack, right after she tells her side, you will have a chance to share what happened from your perspective too. Amy can you tell me what happened during the conflict?

After hearing Amy's side of the story, I say, "Now I would like you to listen to Jack without interrupting while he tells his side of the story. Jack, will you explain step by step what happened during the fight?"

In addition to asking each child to take turns sharing without blaming or accusing, and listening without interrupting, I might also prompt them to think of questions to ask each other to make sure they understand the other person's perspective on the conflict and related feelings. Learning to understand another person's perspective and feelings fuel empathy, a key skill that influences the entire mediation process in beneficial ways. Children may differ greatly in their perspective taking and empathy skills, but children (and adults) can learn through direct modeling and teaching.

C–Clarify Emotions and Interests

During the first steps of mediation, each child has an opportunity to share his or her perspective and feelings about the conflict without interruption. This does not mean they will understand or appreciate what is shared by their siblings. As parent-mediators, we have a key responsibility to help them ask follow-up questions and reflect what they have heard to make sure they understand their siblings' side of the story.

Questions and reflection statements do more than provide evidence of comprehension for the listening. When siblings hear their thoughts and feelings reflected in questions and statements from their siblings, they feel understood and that their personal thoughts and feelings have been recognized. Through clarifying questions and reflection statements, children build empathy and understanding with each other.

Because people have competing interests, high emotion, and conflict history, we all need to learn how to ask clarifying questions so that we truly understand the perspective, thoughts, feelings, and goals of the other person in a conflict. These questions may take a variety of forms, but we must avoid any semblance of judgment or evaluation. Sometimes, children can simply provide a summarizing statement delivered as a reflection of active listening.

Like other communication in this context, the questions we ask should be open-ended, thoughtful, and non-evaluative. Instead of using questions to threaten or shame each other, the goal is to better understand and empathize with each other. The way we ask questions will influence how much children are willing to share during parent-led mediation. In the exercise that follows my examples, you can practice turning shaming questions or statements into clarifying questions or reflection statements.

Examples of Clarifying Questions and Reflection Statements

Ethan has just shouted at Amy for making what he believed to be too much noise in the kitchen while he's trying to do his homework. He feels overwhelmed and stressed about completing the work, but does not want to be away from others while he studies. I sit with Ethan and Amy to help them work out a peaceful solution to their conflict centered around competing interests. Each child has shared their initial perspective, but I help Amy work through asking Ethan a question or making a reflection statement back to him.

Clarifying Questions

To ensure proper understanding of another's perspective and help each person develop empathy, we can guide our children in asking each other clarifying questions. When Ethan began shouting at Amy in the kitchen during homework time, I suggested that Amy ask Ethan the following type of questions:

"Ethan, does it bother you that I'm watching *My Little Pony* while you're trying to do your homework? Is it hard for you to concentrate when I'm watching something on the computer?"

Sometimes, stating the obvious helps to validate the concerns of the conflict parties. But with older children, statements that are too obvious and repetitive may only escalate the feelings of frustration or anger. Gauge the types of questions and statements appropriate for the level of maturity and verbal expression of the parties involved in the conflict.

Reflection Statements

Sometimes, we do not need to ask a clarifying question, but can just make a reflection statement that demonstrates that we have heard the other person. In short, we are checking in to make sure that the intended message has been received. For example, Amy could say the following to Ethan:

"Ethan, I heard you say that it's hard to concentrate when I play the computer while you're doing your homework. Did I understand you correctly?"

Combining Clarifying Questions with Reflection Statements

Combining clarifying questions with reflection statements will help us confirm our findings about the other person and even gain more information, if needed. Amy could make the following reflection statement to Ethan with a clarifying question or request for more information:

"It sounds like you have a hard time concentrating on

your homework when I watch a show in the kitchen. Did I get that right? Is there anything else that makes it hard for you to concentrate on your homework?"

This process may be shortened, but makes a big difference in not only helping the listener receive the proper message, but in letting the other party know that they are understood.

Exercise for Parents: Clarifying Questions and Reflection Statements

Turn these shaming, evaluative questions in *A* into clarifying questions in *B* that allow the other person to let down their defenses and share openly. I provide three examples of alternative clarifying questions among the given *A* statements.

A: Didn't you know that was wrong?

B: I'm wondering how you decided to make the choice to_____. Can you fill me in a little bit about that?

A: What made you say that?

B: Can you tell me more about how you feel about _____?

A: Did you forget what we talked about?

B:

A: How could you do that?

B:

A: Why did you do that?

B: I'm wondering how you decided to _____. Can you fill me in a little bit about that?

A: Why do you always think you're right?

B:

A: What makes you think you can do that?

B:

A: Why are you always trying to go behind my back?

B:

A: Why are you being so selfish?

B:

A: How is that fair to me?

B:

After completing this exercise, consider how you might respond differently to *B* as opposed to *A*. The real test will come when you incorporate these patterns into your daily communications with your family, friends, coworkers, and even strangers. I suggest starting with a small goal of one person you can interact with better. Gradually, you will build up habits that will reflect an overall change in your relationships and not just with one particular person.

Exercise 2: Parents Helping Children Develop Constructive Questions

Write down constructive questions that you or your children ask during the day. Perhaps, you can record them on a whiteboard or paper in your kitchen. Follow up with the next thought: What did you learn about your child or yourself through those questions? Parents could ask their children this same question in a family meeting.

You can practice asking clarifying questions and making reflection statements outside of direct mediation experiences. As these skills become habitual in your daily life, you will more readily incorporate them into more intense problem-solving situations. Children benefit when you use these skills as you interact with them each day. These skills can help you avoid jumping to conclusions and dispensing undue criticism and evaluation of ideas before thoughtfully exploring them. Perhaps, these skills will filter into your other relationships with peers and significant others as well!

H–Hear All Ideas and Reframe Conflict

Sometimes, parents have the tendency to jump toward developing solutions to problems before taking the time to understand the issues and emotions of each child. If you keep a list of issues that each child has shared, you ensure that you've covered what your children care about. Review your list and ask your children to supplement or verify that you've addressed their concerns and emotions in a fair way.

As children share their thoughts and feelings *and* hear their siblings reflect what they hear and understand, they will be better prepared to reframe their conflict as of a joint problem rather than feeling victimized by their siblings. As a parent-mediator, your children will need a lot of initial assistance with reframing conflicts into joint problems because people naturally tend to blame others rather than take responsibility for conflict behavior.

Despite the human tendency to blame others for

conflict, the parent-led mediation process reinforces the joint-problem reframing process because we all talk about each other's perspectives and feelings in a way that provides a wider view of the conflict. Everyone concerned begins to understand that the conflict can be interpreted different ways and that our viewpoint is not the only one. The prior steps of sharing, asking questions, and reflecting prepare children to see beyond themselves and their egocentric interpretations of conflict experiences and feelings.

In several research studies led by Dr. Hildy Ross, professor emerita at the University of Waterloo, children involved with parent-led mediation talked about their own and their siblings' emotions much more often than children in control groups. In fact, older siblings in mediation scenarios placed equal emphasis on their younger sibling's interests and emotions, which goes against common control group tendencies for older siblings to blame younger children and assert their will against the weaker party. Generally, older siblings in the control group were more aggressive, more argumentative, and more likely to blame their younger siblings for conflicts.

Children trained in mediation not only discussed their own emotions more, but could also identify their siblings' goals and emotions more readily. Parents and children discussed emotions when trying to resolve conflicts with each other. When parents provide an arena to talk about emotions, children learn to regulate their feelings more easily and learn empathy for each other; these skills influence their ability to reframe the conflict and decide how to resolve it.

EXERCISES FOR PARENTS

Exercise 1: Listening without Making Evaluative Judgments

Listen and restate what others say to you for a whole day without making an evaluative judgment about the other person's conversation content. What do you need to make this possible? Do you need reminders? An accountability partner? Consider your experience at the end of the day. When was it hard? Where could you improve? What did you learn from the other people you listened to that you did not know before?

Exercise 2: Listing Conflict issues

Think of a conflict situation in your life. Create a list of issues involved in that conflict. For example, when a child does not do his or her homework when asked, there are multiple issues to consider:

- Child may get a poor grade or an immediate punishment like detention.

- Parent must follow up with the teacher about the assignment.

- Child not fulfilling an assignment draws a parent's attention away from other children who may need help.

- Parent feels stressed trying to remember child's assignments in addition to regular duties like cooking dinner, making phone calls, and catching up with other children.

- Child feels nagged and untrusted by the parent.

Reframe the issues so that you address the interests of all parties to the conflict. For this exercise, it's easier to start with a conflict between two people.

If you have chosen a conflict with your spouse or significant other, you'll probably want to let them know what you're doing and ask if they want to participate. See if you can follow the first steps of active listening, then reframe the issues that you have uncovered with each other. Write them down—be formal about it, especially while you're practicing these ideas. If your spouse or partner does not want to participate, you will benefit by creating a personal list of conflict issues and trying to reframe them into joint issues. You will likely learn something about your spouse or partner's perspective in the process.

EXERCISES FOR CHILDREN

Exercise 1: Repeat Back without Evaluative Judgments

Tell your kids a quick story or share a thought with them. Have them practice repeating it back to you without adding any positive or negative judgements about what happens in the story. Encourage them to repeat even the smallest detail when they can. Practice this daily.

Exercise 2: Developing Lists of Conflict Issues

Bring your children together and talk about a pertinent conflict. If a child is old enough, have him or her write down a list of issues that relate to that conflict. Assume the role of scribe if your children are too young to write for themselves.

Check in with each other to make sure that you have truly addressed the needs and interests of all participating parties. Try to keep this very brief with young children, but you can have a fuller discussion with older children. Remember not to get defensive, only listen. As the parent, you are a facilitator here, although you may also be a party to the conflict.

Continuing with H–Hear All Ideas and Reframe Conflict

After making sure that your children have correctly understood the thoughts, feelings, and perspectives of his or her sibling, your role it to reframe what has been shared as a joint problem to be resolved collaboratively. This step often requires more parent input than the other steps because children frequently have a hard time seeing that more than one person is responsible for a conflict. Children naturally focus on their own interests and reasoning, so they may need help in expanding their dialogue to encompass overlapping interests shared between children (think of the child development milestones in chapter 4).

Reframing Conflict into a Jointly-shared Problem

When parents take the time to properly reframe the sibling conflict, they help children avoid blaming, shaming, and complaining about past actions and turn children's stated interests into positive, future-oriented statements that involve joint action with their siblings. Reframing means that you choose to see the current situation from a different perspective to create new patterns in the future. Ask yourself questions like, What kind of solution would help us both get what we need and want in the future?

EXERCISES FOR PARENTS

Exercise 1: Reframe A Statements into Requests for Future Action

A: You spilled the milk again. Will you please stop being so messy!

B: Here. Let's clean up the accident. Next time, will you make sure you pour the milk at the table?

A: Stop fighting with your brother. You're making me crazy!

B: I really want you boys to get along. What would you both enjoy doing together?

A: Why did you miss those two problems on your math test?

B:

A: Can't you ever remember to take the trash out like you're supposed to?

B:

A: Your room is so messy. I can't stand being in
     your room.

B:

A: Did you poop in your pants again? That's so gross.

B:

A: Why didn't anyone close the door? Why am I always
     having to close it when we leave?

B:

A: Be quiet! You guys never listen.

B:

A: Can't you sit still for just one minute?

B:

A: Just eat it. I spent a lot of time making this.

B:

Exercise 2: Turning a Conflict into a Future-Oriented Hope

Think about a current conflict you are experiencing or have recently experienced. How could you reframe that conflict into a future-oriented statement of hope for improvement? (For example, "Your room is a mess, and you haven't done your chores like I asked you to" becomes "I would like you to have a clean room and take care of the chores you have each week.")

EXERCISE FOR CHILDREN

Exercise 1: Reframe Current Negative Statements into Requests for Future Action

Help your children change each negative statement into a future-oriented hope:

- I hate her. She's always taking my stuff.

- He never helps clean up.

- She's lying. I didn't take it.

- Shut up. Your singing is so irritating.

- It's not fair. He always gets playdates.

- I didn't do it. You never believe me.

- I can't. I don't know how.

- She's always saying mean things.

- Stop watching me.

- You made me mess up.

You are the best model of the skill of reframing. You will probably find that your children copy even your choice of words from time to time. When you begin to blame or accuse, rather than stating something you'd really like to have happen in a positive, future-oriented way, catch yourself and start over.

M–Make Joint Decisions

From research and personal experience, I understand that parent intervention is key; otherwise, children rarely work out their conflicts in a way that balances the interests of the older child with the goals and interests of the younger children. In addition, I understand that when parents do intervene to help resolve children's conflicts, we often intervene too heavily and decide outcomes for children.

Despite these non-collaborative tendencies, when you as a parent follow the first five steps of TEACH ME, you make space for ample sharing and exploring of emotions, perspectives, and interests to reframe the conflict as a joint problem to be solved. If you successfully reframe the problem to reflect your children's main goals and interests, you are ready to brainstorm and select a solution that reflects the primary interests of both children.

Brainstorming Solutions

When you ask children to brainstorm potential solutions to their conflicts, you are simply encouraging them to think of as many workable solutions as possible. During this exercise, you may need to remind your kids of the cardinal rule of brainstorming: Get all ideas out before evaluating any of the suggestions. I recommend writing the ideas down for the kids so that they can each see and reflect upon them as they think. If the kids are too young to read, you can read the list to help them remember what they've already included as ideas.

To begin the brainstorming process, ask your children questions like these:

- What ideas can you both think of that would address the things you both want?

- What can you think of that would resolve both people's wants and needs?

- What kinds of solutions would work to help you both get what you want?

Exercise for Parent: Brainstorming Solutions

Consider a current conflict. It's best to use the one you've considered in the previous section for generating an issues list. Without evaluating your own or another's ideas, come up with the longest list you can of possible solutions while concentrating on it for about twenty minutes. Do not cross anything off your list.

It's best to do this with a spouse or significant other regarding a real conflict. Practice your self-control and do not judge anything at this point. You will be surprised at how hard it can be to keep your mouth shut about your ideas, but especially the other party's ideas. It is critical to keep the brainstorming going as long as you can.

Exercise for Parents and Children: Brainstorming Solutions

Reflecting principles shared in Dr. Ross Greene's book *The Explosive Child*, study your child for a few days and figure out what two to three situations provoke outrage or other conflict behavior in your child. During a peaceful, calm moment, talk to your child about that scenario and come up with a plan between you that will address how to resolve that issue. For example, if your three-year-old screams and hits every time his brother grabs his toys, talk about how he might react differently. Small children and many adults often have trouble developing more than one solution to their problem, especially when angry. Waiting until all parties have settled down will help everyone brainstorm multiple solutions to a joint problem.

Once you have a healthy list of ideas, the kids may be ready to evaluate their ideas together—with our guidance. One by one, work through the children's solution list and discuss each child's thoughts, feelings, and perspectives about a given solution.

Before selecting a potential solution, you can help the kids consider possible criteria to use for judging the quality of the solution they select. Your criteria might be as simple as the following:

- The solution must work within general family rules we already have.
- The solution must reflect the main interests of both siblings in conflict.
- The solution must be realistic enough to work in our daily family life.

While you try out parent-led mediation, I want to offer you some encouragement in the form of research. Parent-led mediation studies by Dr. Hildy Ross and her associates suggest that in addition to discussing each other's emotions more often in mediation settings, children also developed a greater variety of solutions that reflected interests of both the younger and older siblings. Oftentimes, the solutions children develop demonstrated greater creativity and were more constructive than parents' ideas that were crafted in control group settings.

In addition, in parent-led mediation studies, both younger and older siblings were more likely to ask a sibling to work with them to find a solution to the conflict and accept discussed plans and restitution by siblings for past wrongs.

Of great significance, in parent-led mediation studies involving children ranging in age from three to eleven, younger siblings developed plans for resolution nearly as often as their older siblings. This result is very different from siblings in control settings. Older siblings generally directed the resolution process and focused on their emotions and interests rather than balancing the emotions and interests of their younger siblings.

Despite this encouraging data from parent-led mediation studies, I have a few warnings for parents about process control during this stage. As children evaluate their lists of potential solutions, you may need to reinforce the basic rules to prevent name-calling, blaming, and possibly even criticizing. You must help your children avoid getting lost in discussion of past wrongs and bad feelings related to the current conflict or any other conflicts from the past.

Also, you may be tempted to steer the discussion toward your favorite or preferred solution. Although you *do* want to control the process to make sure the kids make a wise decision, you *do not* want to decide which solution they apply. You may need to exercise quite a bit of restraint at this point, but it's worth the effort. Instead, you can ask good questions to provide guidance to your young decision makers.

Selecting Solutions

After brainstorming and evaluating ideas based on basic agreed-upon criteria, like family rules, your kids will likely be ready to choose a solution together. This may be a simple solution, like Ben's blanket tent, or it may require a lengthier discussion. During this stage, take the time to make sure that both children agree to a given solution and understand how it will satisfy each person's interests and goals. If attention spans are short, you may need to break up the mediation into smaller sessions and resume discussion when all involved are ready to participate.

Reality Testing Solutions

If your children arrive at a joint decision that both find satisfactory, congratulate and support them. It's exciting when kids finally agree to a solution. But before you quit the process, help your kids to reality test their chosen solution.

Reality testing means asking your children questions about how the solution would work given certain conditions, such as a change in the weather, an increase in homework, sickness, a friend's visit, and so forth. Try to anticipate any obstacles to the success of their chosen solution without beating the idea to death before your children have even had a chance to implement the idea. In short, prepare for potential problems, even if it sounds like a good idea in theory.

You can never anticipate every single possibility related to a potential solution. But, given the depth of family relationships and considerable interaction with each other, you can preview many possibilities before implementing a new solution to a conflict.

For example, during Ben and Amy's fight over the coveted living room spot and blanket, I could have helped the children reality test the tent solution by asking them the following questions:

- What if Amy does not want to build a tent with you?
- What if you both wake up at the same time and want the blanket and the spot then?
- What if someone else in the house wants the blanket when you both want it?

If the Mediation Reaches a Stalemate or Tension Increases

If, despite your high hopes, there is increased tension between your children or a stalemate develops during the decision-making phase, you may need to take breaks or leave off the mediation process. If you reach an impasse, you might ask our children the following questions:

- Is there something about a particular solution that you do like?
- Is there something about the solution your sibling

likes that you do not like or does not work for you?

- How could we change a solution to better fit what you need and what your brother or sister needs?

In the worst-case scenario, you may need to walk away from the mediation attempt without a final solution. Within your family rules, which are discussed in chapter 10, you can provide for a way out of mediation stalemates by determining another appropriate decision-making process (i.e., have a parent decide or have the family counsel together about an appropriate response). You could use other resolution methods, similar to arbitration or litigation, just as you might in adult mediation settings.

Before quitting the mediation process, however, consider that the process can take place in stages if the children are not able to follow through with each step successively in one session. Most importantly, help your children understand that they have choices within the mediation, but if they choose not to participate, they may become subject to another resolution method that is not as collaborative and may involve less freedom and more control by others.

E–Expect Changes

After investing considerable time in the parent-led mediation process, we certainly hope that children choose solutions that will work and be easy to implement in daily life. Sometimes, the solution will work for a while then need to be modified as circumstances, feelings, and thoughts change. Even if the whole process went well and the children came up with a strong solution, we should expect changes. For example, in the war over the cozy, blue blanket, when the weather warms up and my children move outside to play, the possibility for new interactions (and potential conflicts) arise.

Though you'll need to make changes to solutions, remember that other key points of the process that are not "lost" if the solution needs to be modified. Through parent-led mediation, children learn to share their true thoughts and feelings while listening to what their siblings have to say and how they feel. You are teaching active listening, perspective taking, empathy, and patience in communication, which are critical skills in all areas of life.

Even without a specific working decision, children will realize that we take their thoughts, feelings, and communication with each other seriously—it matters to us, so we take the time to teach these skills deliberately, guaranteeing that we will not force a decision on our children. If they choose not to participate, other conflict-management strategies may be explored, but children make the most progress in mediation when they are allowed the freedom to direct how conflicts are resolved. Ultimately, parent-led mediation works best when participation is considered voluntary or elective.

Now that you understand the basic steps of parent-led mediation according to the TEACH ME steps, you are ready to explore examples of conflicts with these steps in mind in chapter 9. Given the unique features of each family, child, and parent, I only scrape the surface of parent-led mediation implementation possibilities there. I'm hopeful that these examples will give you the courage and understanding to begin testing these skills in your own home.

Workbook Questions:

- Do I understand the TEACH ME steps? If so, how would I explain them to someone else?
- Which TEACH ME steps do I find could be effective in my own home?
- Do I believe that I can effectively try to mediate my children's conflicts?
- If I am hesitant, how do I need to prepare myself and my kids to be effective in mediating?

To raise a generation of mediators, we must mediate ourselves. We are parents and not necessarily neutral parties, but we love all our children and can learn skills that will model the behavior we hope they will incorporate in their daily interactions with peers, adults, and family members.

Chapter 8 Summary

What is Mediation?

In mediation, a mediator, or third-party communications assistant, facilitates sharing, listening, brainstorming, and decision-making between two or more parties who are in conflict.

Overview of Parent-Led Mediation

Definition and Purpose

In parent-led mediation, a parent assumes the role of mediator to help two or more children resolve a pressing conflict that parents have deemed intense or significant enough to warrant the time involved in processing the conflict collaboratively.

Roles

As a mediator, the parent controls the communications process of seven basic TEACH ME steps.

As conflict parties, the participating children respect the mediation process and assistance from the parent mediator, but ultimately wield decision-making power to discuss, reflect, brainstorm, select, and evaluate any decision about their conflict with each other.

Basic Parent-Led Mediation Steps

Time to Assess
Establish Structure
Acknowledge Alternate Views
Clarify Emotions and Interests
Hear All Ideas and Reframe Conflict
Make Joint Decisions
Expect Changes

CHAPTER 9
IMPLEMENTING PARENT-LED MEDIATION IN OUR HOMES

Imagine trying to learn how to dance solely by reading about it and watching others. Excellent models do help us learn, but nothing is more effective than feeling how our own bodies move as we attempt to perform the right moves and feel the ebb and flow of energy as we dance with various partners. This goes for us as parents, as well as our children, when we attempt to master new communications skills in both common and less familiar social situations.

In this sense, learning how to mediate is like learning how to dance. Observation and mental study help us only to a certain point. Ultimately, we must step out and try out mediation steps ourselves. To perfect the dance and make it graceful, you would need to practice certain moves over and over again. You start with what you know and add skills as you become more comfortable.

Feeling the music and your response to it means that we go beyond mere imitation of specific techniques. When we seek to help our children resolve conflict, and actually mediate with them, we must cultivate the real feelings of concern and respect for children's freedom of choice. We must care enough to take on the actual attributes of a mediator rather than merely imitate what a mediator does.

Unlike learning algebra, playing Sudoku, or even running a marathon, mediation is more than a solo intellectual or physical exercise. In this communication dance with more than one partner, how much greater is the need for patience and perspective as all dancers find the rhythm and recall the right steps at the right time?

But, what if we want to dance, and the other person does not? It can be awkward to dance alone, but using mediation principles can influence change in social interactions, even without the initial buy-in of a partner or child. Mediation principles may influence change in our relationships even if only one person chooses to dance; if done with sincerity, active listening, acknowledging other points of view, asking clarifying questions, and demonstrating empathy, you create situations of trust and intimacy.

Of course, people can reject us and our approaches, and our children often do. But, both adults and children are much less likely to reject us if we approach them and apply these collaborative communication principles. We model and directly teach mediation principles in the hope that children will imitate our constructive behavior, then gradually gain an understanding of why these principles are useful in their own lives.

What if the dance looks too hard or we feel like we have no skills? We start where we are and take one step at a time—literally. We have learned our current communication skills, including tone of voice, word choice, when to be silent, when to laugh, etc., over many years. We do not throw out everything that we already know and do. We've learned many constructive steps that we can incorporate in parent-led mediation. Certainly, we'll leave some negative habits behind, but our focus is on the positive habits that we already bring to the table.

We bring the communication tools and skills from our prior experience and put them into a new framework to focus on a collaborative approach when appropriate. The TEACH ME mediation steps, alongside a conflict framework, help shape our parent-led mediation success.

Understanding Whether to Dance (Mediate)

As I mention in chapter 8, parent-led mediation is not appropriate for resolving every type of sibling conflict. Instead, parent-led mediation represents a viable option for collaborative conflict resolution to resolve our children's more intense, reoccurring conflicts with each other.

You may not always have a chance to even use all the mediation steps to resolve an appropriate conflict. But, using portions of the mediation process helps children to develop the problem-solving, empathy, and perspective-taking skills that are critical to forming satisfying, lasting interpersonal relationships throughout their lives.

When considering whether you should mediate the sibling conflict at hand, remember the questions developed by Thomas and Kilmann for conflict assessment in chapter 2. After each question, you will find answers in parentheses that lead us toward or away from mediation.

- Is the conflict simple or complex? (More complex.)

- How important is the topic to both persons? (Important to one or more parties.)

- Is there enough time to address the conflict? (Ample time required.)

- Is there enough trust between both people to share their true needs and concerns with one another? (Trust either necessary or desired.)

- Do people have good listening and communication skills? (Developed or at least supported by a parent-led mediator.)

- How important is the relationship to both people, and do they want the relationship to last? (Although siblings may refute the importance of the sibling relationship, parents know that it is important and needs to be nurtured through parental guidance.)

You don't need to answer each of these questions perfectly to choose mediation. But, be aware of gaps in your children's trust, skills, and motivation, which you will need to supplement if you choose to help them mediate. You must ensure a fair process with a decently balanced power structure so no sibling takes advantage of the other. You may not be ready to leap, but you can at least step toward more collaborative approaches.

In this chapter, I look at several different sibling conflict scenarios and show you how I determine whether to mediate or not. Some sibling conflicts require multiple conflict approaches to deal with multifaceted issues. To assist you in making these assessments, I strengthen the analysis with a framework for conflict borrowed from another area of social science.

Identifying Which Factors to Focus on in Our Conflicts

To begin trying out your new skills and move toward parent-led mediation, you might turn to a very practical framework developed by injury prevention expert William Haddon. To prevent injuries, Haddon suggested that we look at factors involved in accidents in three distinct phases: before the event, during the event, and after the event. I use a modified Haddon Matrix to frame a variety of factors involved in the phases of conflict.

Conflict Matrix	Individual Personality and Skills	Relationship Factors	Environmental Factors
Before Conflict			
During Conflict			
After Conflict			

To understand conflict, focus on identifying individual personality, temperament, and conflict management skills along with relationship and environmental factors. Each of these factors influence how you approach your children's conflicts and whether to use mediation skills and processes.

First, examine children's individual personalities, temperament, and conflict management skills. Knowing your children as individuals, you assess the influence of these three categories in pre-conflict, conflict, and post-conflict phases. This structure may seem overly formal, but it provides a mental framework for you as you begin thinking about your children's conflicts.

Individual Personality and Skills Factors

Individual Personality or Temperament:

- Introvert vs. extrovert
- Blame self vs. blame others
- Cautious vs. rash
- Patient vs. impetuous
- Generous vs. stingy
- Self-confident vs. shy
- Calm vs. nervous
- Self-centered vs. focused on others

Communication Skills to Reassess Regularly

To improve our conflict resolution experiences, we should consider regularly reassessing our abilities with the following individual communication skills:

- Share personal feelings and perspectives without blaming or accusations

- Listen to others' feelings and perspectives without interrupting

- Ask clarifying questions and reflect another's stated feelings

- Brainstorm potential solutions to a problem without criticizing others' suggestions

- Discuss the pros and cons of different ideas

- Select a solution that meets their needs as well as the other parties' needs

- Revisit a problem if the chosen solution doesn't seem to be working

With the context of your children's personality and skills in mind, assess the influence of sibling (and parent) relationship factors, including the following:

Relationship Factors

- Sibling ages
- Sibling birth order
- Sibling gender

- Older vs. younger sibling
- Age difference between siblings
- Relative warmth of sibling relationship
- Competition between siblings
- Trust between siblings
- Shared interests with sibling
- Sibling conflict history
- Influence of preferential parent treatment

During your assessment of relationship factors within the three phases, remember that siblings who are closer in age and of the same sex tend to have conflicts more frequently with each other, but they also usually experience greater sibling relationship warmth. Also keep in mind our tendency to intervene more heavily and with a blaming mindset with an older son interacting with a younger sister. Most importantly, avoid the pitfall of demonstrating preferential treatment of one child over another because this corrodes positive parent-child and sibling relationships.

Finally, take key environmental factors seriously and understand that they sometimes prove more influential in conflict than even children's personalities or temperaments. Avoid judging your children's character before evaluating environmental factors, like fatigue, hunger, stress, and even the weather. We all are more influenced by environmental and situational factors than we'd like to believe.

Environmental Factors

- Time constraints

- Individual and family stress

- Body temperature

- Noisy vs. quiet

- Crowded vs. isolated

- Time of day

- Familiar vs. unfamiliar location

- Employment responsibilities

- Type of weather (hot vs. cold, humid vs. dry, rainy vs. sunny)

- Hungry vs. full

- Tired vs. rested

- Financial situation

- Physical or mental health vs. illness

By identifying key conflict factors, you can choose an active, conscious approach to conflict rather than hoping a conflict will resolve itself, which rarely happens in regular life. Using this matrix and the six questions presented in chapter 8, you can begin to distinguish when you should or shouldn't intervene as mediator in your children's conflicts.

You will gain clarity as you reflect on conflict within this simple framework. In fact, understanding the interplay of these three different types of factors during the three phases of before, during, and after conflict will help us with all the conflicts we encounter in our different relationships. In the end, this same conflict matrix may guide us toward understanding when we should avoid, accommodate, compromise, collaborate, or even compete.

Workbook Questions:

- What do I think of the conflict matrix?
- Does the matrix make sense to me? What don't I understand about it? What would I change?
- Are there any factors I would add to the individual, relationship, and environmental factors already mentioned?
- How could the conflict matrix be useful in my own life?
- How could the conflict matrix influence my parenting?

Using the Conflict Matrix to Understand Your Potential Approaches

Getting Rats vs. a Rat

Emma, and my middle son, Jack, both love animals. Also, they both enjoy being identified as animal lovers, or being described as "the nature kid." Often, over the years, they have had conflicts over the coveted identity as the Taylor family's sole nature or animal lover.

In this ongoing conflict scenario, both children seem to believe that only one child can be identified as the nature lover. In this sense, an identity within the family is perceived as a limited or contested resource. Somehow, we need to deal with this perception of a finite possibility for identity within the family. Is it possible that we could have two Taylor family nature or animal lovers?

This conflict has arisen around family pets. My husband and I had allowed Jack to choose two of our first pets, a leopard gecko and a desert lizard, who have since joined our front yard pet cemetery. While we have wanted to give Emma a pet, we haven't been ready for the larger animal that she desires, like a dog.

Last year, when Jack's birthday rolled around, I wanted to avoid unnecessary conflict about giving one child a pet over another. Jack seemed very excited about getting a small pet, like another lizard, but as parents, we already knew that we needed to avoid the appearance of preferential treatment.

Birthday gifts may bring happiness to one child, but any show of preferential treatment can be detrimental to the sibling relationship and create all kinds of sibling and parent-child conflict. In this case, we had a few factors to consider before deciding what to do about adding pets to our household.

Here I review a prior conflict over the leopard gecko, Spots, who died under Jack's watch. Emma often reminds us of this incident when discussing if we would get another family pet.

Conflict Matrix	Individual Personality and Skills	Relationship Factors	Environmental Factors
Before Conflict: Before Spots' Death	Emma is more verbal and aggressive. Jack is sensitive and more forgetful about pet care maintenance.	Emma is the older sister. Jack is younger and less verbal. They do not enjoy close sibling relationship; limited warmth compared to other sibling pairs in the family	Mom is allergic to cats and not open to getting a dog. There is a leopard gecko living in Jack's room. Friends are interested in holding and playing with the gecko.
During Conflict: Spot Dies	Jack feels deep remorse about the accident that caused Spots' death. Emma feels deep compassion for animals and cannot understand Jack's neglect.	Emma is the older, more mature sibling. She readily perceives what happens and tells the family about the neglect and lack of care. Jack is quieter and deeply saddened about losing a pet.	Busy household with ongoing demands. No one noticed that Spots was caught under his stone covering. Spots lived in Jack's room, so there is not much oversight by others.

After Conflict: Spots has died	Emma makes accusations and cries for her oversight over any future pets.	Emma and Jack prepare Spots' grave, but Emma takes the lead in the ceremonies.	We already have all the equipment to house another gecko or lizard, but wonder if that's still the best option.

To Mediate or Not?

Rather than mediating, I decided to do some investigation into the best pets for kids and reflect on this serious conflict history between my two animal-loving children. While lizards were easy to maintain, they were not as interactive as my children desired. I acknowledged that I kept accommodating Jack's interest in animals because he enjoyed reptiles, which I could tolerate in the home. I also realized that I was unwittingly demonstrating preferential treatment for Jack and avoiding Emma's demand for a pet of her own because she wanted a pet that I did not want and that we weren't ready to manage as a family.

In short, I had fueled a sibling conflict by allowing Jack to enjoy having a pet while Emma had to somehow watch this preferential treatment as a bystander. As I came to realize how unfair my actions had been, I reframed their conflict as a joint problem to be solved: How could I satisfy both Jack's and Emma's love for animals and their mutual desire to have pets of their own?

Through gathering information about various types of

good pets for children, I happened upon the rat. Yes, the rat. Although I am not particularly fond of rodents in the wild, everything I read convinced me that rats made great pets for children: they're clean, smart, sociable, and even able to learn simple commands. Rather than compromising on an animal I did not want to take care of, like a dog, I imagined a scenario in which both Emma and Jack could take care of smaller animals together.

When Jack's birthday rolled around, I offered to get both Emma and Jack one rat each—making sure that we got two females so that they wouldn't eat each other (we had been warned about the potential for male rats to duke it out until one rat survived).

In this case, I did do a lot of investigating, talking, and preparing for resolution to an ongoing conflict, but I first investigated my own patterns of behavior alongside the three areas related to Emma and Jack's earlier conflicts about pets. In short, I chose not to mediate but to rework our existing situation in which parental preferences fueled conflict between my children. Interestingly, many months later, while Emma still needs to remind Jack to play with his pet rat Charlotte, they both have opportunities to love and care for animals in a sustainable way without heavy conflict. Overall, taking care of the rats helped us prepare for the puppy we eventually got for the entire family.

Purchasing, Comparing, Trading, and Expanding on Pokémon Card Collections

Although I detest watching my boys turn over their hard-earned cash from chores to buy booster packs of Pokémon cards at Target, I am thankful for the lessons we have learned through purchasing, comparing, trading, and expanding the card collections. These cards represent my boys' most precious possessions, which they choose to regularly barter and bicker over. I believe the key is that the boys actually own the cards, which allows them to trade for themselves.

It's strange to say this, but I'm thankful for Pokémon cards because they provide opportunities to have and work through numerous conflicts over fairness, negotiation terms, and earning of money to save up to buy more Pokémon cards.

In my boys' world, Pokémon cards are the great elixir of excitement, social status, and achievement. Somehow, these cards provide something my boys are looking for that I am not interested in. However, I am learning to appreciate the cards' importance because many boys (and men) around the world seem to share this Pokémon fetish. I might get excited about a new pair of shoes, but the boys love these cards.

In the early days of purchasing, comparing, trading, and expanding their Pokémon card collections, my oldest son, Ethan, finagled a trade with my youngest son, Ben, for the most powerful Pokémon card, the Primal Kyogre. While Ethan rejoiced in his trading triumph, Ben felt duped and grew angry as he realized how much he wanted to have the Primal Kyogre card back in his possession.

As a parent, I could belittle the importance of these paper cards when there are children that endure real hardships like starvation, war, and abuse around the world. But, in my sons' worlds, these cards represent a type of currency, power, and worth that they are learning to negotiate even in small ways daily.

I chose to evaluate this specific conflict between Ethan and Ben because even a few weeks did not lessen the sting Ben felt from the experience and his feelings of conflict about the loss of his favorite card.

Conflict Matrix	Individual Personality and Skills	Relationship Factors	Environmental Factors
Before Conflict	Ethan was rigid and determined to have the best cards. Ben was eager, competitive, and wanting to interact with his older brothers.	Ethan, as the older brother, was more familiar with Pokémon card values and able to negotiate more fully. Ben was subject to Ethan's knowledge and goodwill.	All three boys were busy trading cards with each other for an extended period of time.

| During Conflict | Ethan believed he'd traded fairly, but Ben didn't know the value of the cards. Ethan didn't have a way to determine value either, although he seemed more aware of possible values. | Ethan pushed heavily for the cards he wanted, and Ben trusted that Ethan was giving him a good deal. | Ben had just received the coveted card the morning of the trade in a new pack, so he didn't know the full value of it. Later that day, Ben realized that he had made a bad trade. |
| After Conflict | Ethan felt justified because he traded other valuable cards for Primal Kyogre. Ben felt angry and used by his older brother. | Ben felt betrayed by Ethan because he believed that Ethan had traded in good faith. | Ben learned what the card was worth after checking prices and values on eBay. He found out what Primal Kyogre was actually worth (more than he traded it for). |

To Mediate or Not?

Given that the conflicts surrounding my sons' trading were ongoing and reoccurring, I decided to mediate Ben and Ethan's conflict with separate conflict coaching and fact gathering.

To make sure that I understood the conflict properly

and to calm negative feelings, I spent some time with each boy separately to hear what had happened. I needed to orient myself in the conflict and show to both boys that I cared about their thoughts and feelings. After getting a good feel for the source of the conflict, as I share in the prior conflict matrix, I attempted to bring the boys together to talk about the conflict once their negative feelings had subsided somewhat.

Each boy shared his side of the story and said what he wanted to have happen. Ben firmly demanded that Ethan return his card, and Ethan said that he'd made a fair trade and that he would not reverse the deal. I reminded them both that they would probably be making a lot more trades with each other in the future and they needed to come up with some ground rules for trades to avoid these problems in the future.

Although we managed to get through perspective sharing and reflecting emotions, the boys needed help asking each other clarifying questions because talking about the conflict escalated Ben's emotions again. I chose to take a break from the parent-led mediation and asked Ethan, specifically, to think about how he would feel if he had just traded Primal Kyogre for the cards he gave Ben. I did not force the issue, but raised the question to help motivate him to reflect on Ben's feelings.

Later in the day, I asked Ethan about what he and Ben had figured out concerning the coveted Primal Kyogre card. Ethan looked surprised by my question and said, "Oh, I already took care of that and offered Ben some more good cards." Ethan had not returned the desired card, but he had worked out a compromise by offering Ben more good cards for the trade.

For the moment, the conflict seemed resolved. Weeks later, Ben reopened the issue by demanding Primal Kyogre back. Further investigation into pricing for this certain card on eBay had fueled Ben's ire. He wanted justice, even though they had worked out an arrangement after the initial conflict. Because this conflict resurfaced (remember, we have to prepare to change if needed), we needed to beef up our Pokémon trading policies through further discussion.

Of note, although eBay helped the boys determine the value of different Pokémon cards, those values do not remain static, but vary depending on the seller and how many buyers are looking for a certain card. Now, before the boys trade cards, they check out pricing on eBay so they are more certain about what is fair and what is not. As I mentioned in chapter 1, people often need to agree about what information counts in a conflict. When it comes to Pokémon cards, making sure all parties understand the relative value and price is an important factor in reducing conflict when purchasing and trading cards between three energetic boys.

In the weeks and months that followed, we had several more conversations about trading Pokémon cards, although the boys have now moved on to other activities like watching Dude Perfect sports stunts.

The Chromebook

As I discuss in chapter 5 on sibling conflict, many conflicts erupt around family privileges and the rules regarding them. In our home, screen time is considered a privilege that must be earned according to strict rules unless a child is working on homework. Each child can earn screen time by practicing their musical instrument. If they choose to practice in the morning, they can earn five extra minutes on the computer. If they choose not to practice their instruments, they don't earn computer time. Everyone understands these rules and follows them with only occasional exceptions.

Although my husband and I have personal computers, my five children have been sharing one Chromebook for twenty minutes of computer time per child per day. If two or more children finish practicing their instruments at the same time, they must figure out who goes first on the computer. Often, conflicts arise when they have to decide who gets to use the computer first. Although my husband and I have offered our computers for twenty minutes of screen time, the children tend to prefer the Chromebook.

To fill out the conflict matrix, I use a younger and older child to unravel how sibling conflicts over the Chromebook unravel on a regular basis.

Conflict Matrix	Individual Personality and Skills	Relationship Factors	Environmental Factors
Before Conflict	An older child demands computer time. A younger child demands computer time.	The older child is larger and more verbal. The younger child is less verbal and more prone to crying or whining to get parent intervention.	Computer time usually takes place after school or during dinner prep. I rarely want to deal with conflicts during these busy hours.
During Conflict	The older child pleads his or her case more effectively while the younger child cries.	Each child expresses how the other child never waits his or her turn and always tries to go ahead.	The kids are usually tired, hungry, and needing to relax.

After Conflict	The older child tries to work in computer time without following the rules because they can get on the computers themselves. The younger child still tries to follow the rules because they can't type in the passwords, but complains heavily to a parent if the older sibling tries to manipulate him or her.	The older child tries to go around the rules with the parent. The younger child tries to get Mom or Dad to enforce the rules with the older child.	Parents are not as vigilant during early morning and later hours. The older children are more likely to use and extend computer time during early morning and late evening hours.

To Mediate or Not?

We could try to mediate the computer use between two children, but most of the rules are fairly clear-cut. For the most part, the kids fight because they want access to a limited or contested resource: the Chromebook. There's not much to mediate beyond who goes first because the twenty-minute time allowance is standard for all the kids. What we really needed to negotiate was what to do when more than one person had earned the privilege and wanted the Chromebook.

As a holiday gift, my husband bought a second Chromebook to ease the fighting over computer time. But, the addition of a second Chromebook did not immediately ease the problem because my kids all wanted to use the familiar computer that held their passwords. We offered some incentives, but nothing too enticing; for example, we gave them five extra minutes if they needed to wait for someone.

About the second Chromebook, I don't necessarily believe we should give in and try to erase all opportunities for our children to learn how to wait and to share a limited resource. But, as my husband expected, adding another Chromebook has nearly eliminated all waiting for computer time because my children tend to stagger their practice and screen times throughout the afternoon and evening.

Adding another device created the additional challenge of my supervising screen time. I find that I now catch my kids watching a lot more Dude Perfect and Studio C videos than our family rules allow. We have yet to manage this new conflict, even though the first conflict about managing screen time turn taking has been generally resolved by expanding a limited resource.

Grumpy Mornings with Amy

It usually takes two to tango when it comes to conflict, but one person can ignite a whole series of conflicts based on nothing more than grumpiness, a bad attitude, or just plain immaturity. Many mornings, I watch my tired five-year-old try to incite her siblings with all kinds of accusations and crying. Sometimes, she is in a foul mood after waking up. It's possible that her age makes it harder to regulate her emotions and manage self-control when she is tired, hungry, or not feeling social.

On one school morning, Amy targeted her morning

angst at her oldest brother, Ethan, who was quietly eating his breakfast at the kitchen table. Even with a sudden, random eruption of conflict, we turn to the conflict matrix to understand how to handle the apparent fight.

Conflict Matrix	Individual Personality and Skills	Relationship Factors	Environmental Factors
Before Conflict	Amy tends to sleep longer than Ethan and wakes up more slowly. She has a hard time reining in emotion. Ethan is an early riser and is generally chipper in the morning.	Amy and Ethan tend to tease and love each other intensely—kind of a hot-cold relationship. As her older brother, Ethan does provoke Amy, but she tends to provoke him too.	It is morning. Amy is hungry. Ethan is at the table eating and is calmly sitting at the table when Amy arrives.
During Conflict	Amy begins complaining about being woken up, about how loud people are and then begins shouting; she spirals upward without the natural ability to de-escalate on her own.	Ethan is annoyed that he has been targeted. Amy is on the defensive because she is often picked on by her older siblings.	The rest of the family is calm and have already eaten. Amy has newly arrived in a foul mood.

After Conflict	Ethan stays calm. Amy remains upset.	Ethan and the other children feel somewhat defensive because Amy lashed out at all of them and me.	Amy still has not eaten. She is not dressed and remains tired. She has the pressure to get ready for school.

To Mediate or Not?

Amy woke up ready to pick a fight with anyone she encountered. She reacted strongly to a benign remark Ethan made. While I attempted to ask Amy what was bothering her and helped her express her feelings, she did not offer anything productive to the discussion. Instead, her angry mood started to evoke feelings of resentment and anger in the rest of the kids. I started to feel annoyed after making many attempts to smooth things over as she lashed out at Ethan.

Rather than try to mediate this situation, I chose to separate Amy from the rest of the kids. This conflict arose from how Amy was feeling, and I hoped it would end by helping her regain her bearings. She seemed tired and out of sorts, so I needed to focus on helping her adjust and get ready, instead of trying to sort out why she was mad at Ethan. I don't think that she was mad at Ethan specifically because she lashed out at everyone in the same, tired, emotional way.

In this case, separation allowed the flames of conflict to slowly fade away before creating a more real and volatile sibling conflict between Amy and Ethan or any other of her siblings who were present. I found no need to mediate in this conflict situation instigated by one hot-headed party.

Ethan Collecting Coins

Ethan delved into a new hobby for five months: coin collecting. Wherever we went, Ethan sought to collect coins from anyone we encountered. This meant searching for "good" coins at the grocery store, at Chinese class, throughout our neighborhood, and in my purse.

Coin collecting took a lot of our time in public places, especially when Ethan found someone with a large jar of hundreds of pennies, nickels, and quarters to sift through. Most of my children enjoyed helping Ethan sift through coins, but Emma found Ethan's coin collecting both boring and somewhat embarrassing.

One school night, after dragging the kids through a local grocery store after visiting an elderly friend in a nursing home, Ethan asked the check-out clerk about coins. A customer overheard Ethan's question and offered to go retrieve a jar from her car in the parking lot.

Conflict Matrix	Individual Personality and Skills	Relationship Factors	Environmental Factors
Before Conflict	Emma is conscientious about homework, verbal, and completely uninterested in collecting coins. Ethan is very focused and excited to add coins to his collection. It's difficult to stop an activity midstream, especially with a one-time opportunity with this person.	As the oldest child, Emma is unafraid to state likes and dislikes with her younger brother. She is somewhat domineering verbally. Ethan gets annoyed, but mostly stays quiet with her to avoid escalating her feelings.	It is a school night, getting late and dark, the kids are tired, and we've already visited an elderly friend in a nursing home.
During Conflict	Emma used verbal aggression to gain her desired outcome. Ethan ignored her and focused solely on the coins. This escalated Emma's feelings of hostility.	Emma and Ethan share many divergent interests. Ethan generally shows respect for Emma's interests, but Emma tends to show less respect for Ethan's hobbies.	Shoppers pass by all around us. We search through coins on the floor. A developmentally delayed clerk shares lengthy stories with us.

After Conflict	Ethan wishes he had more time to sift through the coins, but he is happy. Emma is completely frustrated and stressed about her homework.	Ethan is still not focused on Emma's thoughts or feelings. Emma is indignant that the entire family took time to sort through coins for Ethan.	We return home later than expected. It was dark, and everyone was tired. Our normal school-night routine was off.

To Mediate or Not?

While I felt exhausted myself, this situation in the grocery store on a school night demanded an on-the-spot, ad hoc parent-led mediation. I knelt on the floor by a tower of fruits and vegetables with coins spread out on the floor. My children knelt around me while a store clerk and the woman with the coin jar discussed the joys of coin collecting. Emma stood near the exit with an angry expression on her face that reinforced her continued appeal to leave immediately.

I bounced back and forth between Ethan and Emma, trying to help them work out their dilemma together, while Ethan sat sorting coins and the clerk and woman swapped stories about the joys of coin collecting. I explained to Emma that we needed to help Ethan collect some of these coins quickly so she could get home to do her homework. In short, they depended on each other to get what they each wanted.

Because Ethan was so focused on collecting coins, I had to act as his intermediary so Emma had someone to collaborate with about her concerns. As Emma and I discussed how to expedite the process, she offered to join in sorting the coins. Eventually, all of us (five kids and me) created a collaborative coin-sorting tactic to look through the finds efficiently. We set a time limit to ensure that we would not arrive home at an unacceptable hour, and with Emma's help and collaboration, we managed to increase the pace considerably.

Although my process was in no way a formal or precise application of the TEACH ME mediation guidelines, we managed to turn an emotional standoff into a collaborative, working solution to meet everyone's needs. Ethan no longer collects coins, but I'm sure other hobbies will interfere with our group dynamics and individual desires. Each time we work together to solve a problem, like the coin sorting, I sense we are creating family unity and patterns for effective communication in the future.

Now What?

From these sibling conflict examples, it's clear that we don't need a collaborative mediation approach in each of these circumstances. We approach different conflicts with a five-approach tool bag of skills. We might choose to avoid, accommodate, compete, compromise, or collaborate in any of these situations based on the circumstances and our assessment of the situation. As parents, we also might need to change things up ourselves, rather than merely expecting our children to modify their behavior and approaches.

I share the whole mediation process here, but you can

start small and build upon your successes in improving communication and conflict management in the home. You can focus on one particular area, even something as simple as getting more sleep (whether for you or the children).

To practice, use the conflict matrix and workbook questions below to describe and analyze a current or recent conflict between two or more of your children.

Workbook Questions:

- Which conflict between my children would I like to address?
- What factor(s) stands out to me?
- Is there something I can do to influence how this factor plays out between my children?
- Is this conflict complex, reoccurring, or infused with stress?
- Does parent-led mediation seem appropriate for helping my children problem solve this conflict?

Start with Small Personal Conflict Management Goals as Parents

Some circumstances we identify in the conflict matrix are easier to influence than others. For example, we can't change other people's personalities or quickly modify a key interpersonal relationship. But, I can focus on environmental factors, such as timing, temperature, hunger, fatigue, and so forth, to prevent predictable conflict scenarios.

On a personal note, one basic way that my husband and I often run into conflicts with each other and sometimes with the children is by not coordinating our schedules with each other. We get overbooked, but we also forget to tell each other about concerts, carpools, work travel, church assignments, and so on. By taking the time to review our calendars together, we avoid a lot of conflicts that result from not planning. For us, the best time to schedule our activities is during a weekly family meeting on Sunday afternoons.

Rather than look for a complicated solution, we should first consider calendaring with each other; we might just need to coordinate, simplify, and talk with each other more about what we're doing on a daily, weekly, and monthly basis. We can restructure the home environment so it's easier to prevent misunderstandings and behave more peacefully with each other.

Some of our family issues are beyond overscheduling or not coordinating activities with each other. They revolve around the need to respect basic communication principles: listening, using a calm, respectful tone of voice, not interrupting, asking thoughtful questions, reflecting what we hear, empathizing with others, brainstorming solutions, and collaborating to face difficult challenges together. These core interpersonal skills mesh to form positive communication patterns that strengthen our relationships inside and outside of the home.

Start with Small Family Communication Goals

In reviewing the mediation steps of TEACH ME, notice that mediation combines a variety of communication skills in one conflict-resolution process.

- Time to Assess
- Establish Structure
- Acknowledge Alternate Views
- Clarify Emotions and Interests
- Hear All Ideas and Reframe Conflict
- Make Joint Decisions
- Expect Changes

These communication skills enhance our ability to resolve conflict in our homes. But trying to implement them all at once with parent-led mediation may seem very overwhelming. To avoid becoming overwhelmed or discouraged, choose small family communication goals. You want to start with small goals that are meaningful and achievable within your family life so that everyone gains confidence in the process.

You can select your small communication goals to support the TEACH ME steps of mediation. The steps are based on the following six basic communication skills. If you're not ready to mediate officially and sit down together in a formal process, you can pick one or more of these skills and work on them specifically.

- Share personal feelings and perspectives without

blaming or accusations.

- Listen to others' feelings and perspectives without interrupting.

- Ask clarifying questions.

- Brainstorm potential solutions to a problem without criticizing others' suggestions.

- Discuss the pros and cons of different ideas.

- Talk about which solutions match the needs and wants of both parties.

In my own home, we are currently focused on developing the first two listed skills: (1) sharing personal feelings and perspectives without blaming or accusations and (2) listening without interruption. Despite my desire to go big, I try to tackle our conflicts and seek solutions in small, doable increments. As parents, we need insight into which communications skills to focus on teaching and how to pace what we teach depending upon our family needs.

For example, I feel grateful for the progress we've made when I hear Amy calmly say, "Please don't interrupt me, it's my turn to talk," rather than screaming and melting down if someone cuts her off while she talks. To help my children express what they feel and to learn to share their perspectives, I often ask them simply, "What do you need right now?"

Asking, What Do You Need Right Now?

The other day, Ethan kept shouting at Ben to be quiet. When I asked him what he needed, Ethan finally said, "I need it to be quiet." We then discussed how the kitchen is a common, public place where we can't expect quiet, so if he needs quiet, he might need to find another place that will better meet his needs. We actually discussed his needs, which he ably expressed to me. To me, this is real improvement for our home environment.

Accepting and Learning from Failure

When you start something new, especially as a lone, motivated parent, it helps to have a growth mindset and to accept failure as part of the process. You start with the hope that family relationships can be improved. Then, you confront the good, the bad, and the ugly of conflict management through the trial and error of new strategies. Eventually, as you and our children master new skills, you gain confidence that positive change is possible.

Concerning conflict failures, research confirms that children benefit from reviewing past conflicts that did not necessarily end well. As you review an unresolved or poorly-resolved conflict, you can discuss how you would do things differently next time with added skills and perspective. This type of conscious teaching and learning prepares us to improve how we handle future conflicts. Essentially, you prepare yourself and your children in times of calm to handle conflicts constructively so that when emotions run high and brains shutdown, you have an action plan to follow.

Catering Parent-Led Mediation Assistance to Children's Ages and Development

Age-Appropriate Mediation Assistance

As you consider your children and how to approach them with the mediation process and principles, realize that the age, gender, and skills of each child affect how and what you teach them about mediation. You may need to provide individual children with tailored communication coaching before attempting mediation with siblings. Make these choices based on your knowledge of family dynamics, personalities and temperaments, and your time and energy to actively implement these skills in your daily lives.

Preschool Children with a Parent-Mediator

With preschoolers, children who are three to six years old, focus on actively participating in the mediation process as a parent mediator. Understand that preschoolers have significant social development milestones to reach, such as the ability to stop an activity midstream and to consider multiple interpretations of an ambiguous conflict. Given their less mature social and intellectual skills and more limited verbal expression, you scaffold the mediation process as needed. Avoid overcompensating for a younger or less mature sibling's attributes to avoid being considered unfair or biased in any way. Help the younger child express their thoughts, but do not defend or evaluate the worth of the younger child's thoughts against an older child. (Preferential treatment of one child over another may damage sibling relationships.)

Try to follow all the TEACH ME mediation steps, but ask for clarifications as needed and refer to the standard rules and process if one or more children get off track. You may need to shorten and modify the process as well, because younger children have shorter attention spans. Despite these modifications, try not to talk on behalf of your children. You nurture young children's abilities to express their thoughts and feelings and help them learn to reflect what their siblings have said when you model this behavior and remind them of the process.

Most importantly, as parent mediators, make sure to help children reframe their issues into jointly-shared problems to solve. Well-framed joint conflicts will allow for the development of better future-based solutions. You want your children to realize the need to cooperate through their jointly-framed interests and goals.

School Aged Children with a Parent Mediation Trainer

You may still need to provide a significant presence in sibling mediation among six- to twelve-year-olds, especially if you are just beginning parent-led mediation at home. But, you might view yourself more as a trainer than full mediator with school-aged children. Your role is to help set up the mediation process and support your kids throughout, but try to turn the reins over to them as much as possible.

Once your six- to twelve-year-olds have mastered the TEACH ME mediation principles, you can gradually withdraw assistance. Remain on deck to help as needed, but trust that, in most cases, children will develop independence in their problem-solving processes. In research settings, children effectively mediated conflicts without their parents present nearly seven months after first learning mediation strategies directly from their parents.

You can also involve your children in determining whether mediation would be appropriate for resolving certain types of sibling conflicts. Over time, your children will learn to decide which conflicts merit collaboration and which issues should be resolved with other conflict management approaches. These experiences choosing appropriate conflict resolution strategies will lead children toward developing conflict fluency, the ability to flexibly respond to conflict with appropriate approaches and attitudes.

Of course, certain sibling relationships won't allow for increased independence from direct parent intervention during mediation (or conflict). When certain sibling pairs fight about hot conflict topics (and even hurt each other), you may need to be just as engaged with your six- to twelve-year-olds as you would with preschoolers. Understand your unique family situation, but attempt to keep mediation voluntary, collaborative, and future-oriented. Don't pressure children into solutions they do not accept or cannot effectively carry out.

Adolescents with a Parent Coach

Most research of adolescents using mediation principles focuses on peer mediation. These studies demonstrate that most adolescents are equipped to learn and use mediation principles to solve conflicts with their peers collaboratively. Adolescents develop a variety of effective communication skills through participating in peer mediation training programs.

However, adolescents have not been studied in mediation studies focused on sibling conflicts; consequently, parent-led mediation's usefulness among this demographic remains unconfirmed. Hopefully, in the future, researchers will document the effect of parent-led mediation in resolving sibling conflicts between adolescents. We simply do not know if adolescents will mediate with their siblings effectively under parental guidance.

Given this gap in research, you might consider less direct methods of parent intervention in sibling conflicts with adolescents. Rather than insert ourselves as parent-mediators, consider gently nudging children in the right direction through one-on-one conflict coaching. In the role of coach, assume that your teenagers still have room to grow in skills and perspective, but respect their autonomy to problem solve with their peers independently.

Given adolescents' growing maturity, extensive verbal ability, and increased capacity for abstract thinking, they likely have the necessary skills to use mediation principles to resolve sibling conflicts. Whether your adolescent children will apply these attributes to resolve conflicts with their siblings must still be determined. Before formal research catches up, you can begin the experiment in your home laboratory with teenage children.

Keeping Perspective on Implementing New Skills and Processes in the Home

As you consider children's conflicts with each other, take the time to assess the situation, especially at first. If you take time up front to understand the personality, temperament and skills, relationship, and environmental factors that influence children before, during, and after conflicts with each other, you will better identify when parent-led mediation is appropriate.

Given the amount of trial and error involved in implementing parent-led mediation, I say, "If at first you don't succeed, try, try again." Any honest and sincere effort we make to teach children problem-solving, perspective taking and empathy skills will not be lost despite some ambiguous or downright failed outcomes. Even truly undesirable results may give us renewed perspective and the contrast needed to better understand children and how to relate to them more effectively. In short, contrasting experiences give us insight into what we're doing well and where we can still improve.

Chapter 9 Summary

Sibling Conflict Demands Flexibility of Approach
When implementing parent-led mediation, recognize that all five general conflict management approaches have a place in our parenting conflict resolution tool belt.

Start with Small Personal Communication Goals
Identify an area of personal conflict management improvement as a parent.

Start with Small Family Communications Goals
Pick one of the skills from the basic conflict management skills to work on as a family:

- Share personal feelings and perspectives without blaming or accusing.
- Listen to others' feelings and perspectives without interrupting.
- Ask clarifying questions.
- Brainstorm potential solutions to a problem without criticizing others' suggestions.
- Discuss the pros and cons of different ideas.

- Select a solution that meets our needs, as well as the other parties' needs.

Conflict Matrix based on Haddon

Conflict Matrix	Individual Personality and Skills	Relationship Factors	Environmental Factors
Before Conflict			
During Conflict			
After Conflict			

Catering Parent-Mediation Assistance to Children's Ages and Development

- Preschoolers (3–5) with a parent-mediator
- School-aged Children (6–12) with a parent-mediation trainer
- Adolescents (13–18) with a parent coach

·

CHAPTER 10
FAMILY PRACTICES THAT SUPPORT PARENT-LED MEDIATION

There is an old Japanese saying, "Kiki naru kikai," which means that "a crisis may become an opportunity." Family conflict often feels more like a crisis, and less like a welcome opportunity. However, sibling conflict may provide enough friction and motivation for us to reconsider our current family patterns. As parents, we can transform this crisis into an opportunity to strengthen our family relationships and deliberately teach critical life skills to our children.

While this book has focused on developing parent-led mediation, four fundamental family practices will assist you in implementing parent-led mediation in your home. These four family practices include the following:

1. Building Parent Communication Skills
2. Holding Regular Family Meetings
3. Establishing and Upholding Family Rules

4. Practicing Clear and Compassionate Communication

We already recognize that children tend to imitate our behavior, positive and negative patterns, words, and expressions. Ultimately, we are our children's most influential teachers and guides toward learning everyday social behavior and communication. We know we must practice what we preach if we hope to have our children to follow the good advice we share with them.

To teach children constructive communication, we begin by modeling effective communication in our daily lives. Do we resolve conflicts with our spouse or significant other in constructive ways? Do we follow the advice we give our children to work out differences fairly and peacefully? Whether we like it or not, every day we lead with our active examples how children should treat each other and anyone else they encounter.

Given the necessity to model the kind of positive behavior we hope our children will adopt, we may need to make changes in our own communication approaches and habits. You may find that small changes (e.g., withholding judgment, responding calmly to a screaming child, and allowing others to express their true feelings and needs) will produce significant changes in the depth and strength of your family relationships. It's true that parents and children need to implement changes to manage conflict, but when parents take the lead and model positive communication behavior, all our family relationships will benefit and strengthen.

Building Parent Communication Skills

Parent Behaviors Can Support or Detract from Successful Parent-Led Mediation

Many intuitive parenting behaviors support the success of parent-led mediation in the home. Likewise, common negative parenting behaviors can decrease the likelihood of successful conflict management using parent-led mediation.

Given our natural tendencies and the need to develop constructive communication skills, I want to share lists of positive and negative behaviors so you can cultivate communication skills that support parent-led mediation.

- Help your children not to blame each other (and avoid blaming one or both children yourself).

- Help your children see how his or her sibling feels about the conflict and in general.

- Help your children think of solutions to their conflicts.

- Help your children say what each child wanted from the conflict.

- Help your children decide about how the fight should be resolved.

- Help your children to make sure that both children are happy with the chosen solution.

You may notice that some of these positive behaviors for settling sibling conflicts come naturally to you, while other behaviors or tendencies will require some learning and effort to develop more fully. As you practice these positive communication behaviors, they will become more natural and instinctual to you, but don't expect overnight transformation in others or yourself.

As a Samoan proverb says, "If you want to go fast, go alone. If you want to go far, go together." If it's your intention to go far together as a family, you need to incorporate more of these positive behaviors in your general family life. And all family members benefit from *avoiding* several behaviors that detract from our ability to resolve conflicts collaboratively:

- Deciding how your children's conflicts should be resolved.
- Yelling at your children for fighting.
- Ignoring your children while they are experiencing conflict.
- Punishing your children for fighting.
- Getting angry with your children when they fight.
- Taking sides when your children are fighting.
- Telling your children to work out the fight themselves.

You may find yourself yelling at your children or punishing them for fighting. It happens. But, the moment you start noticing what we're doing and the negative outcomes that may result, you set yourself up for progress. The next time you start yelling at your kids to stop fighting (or engaging in any other counterproductive behavior), you make the effort to exercise a bit more restraint because you are aware of your behavioral patterns and choices.

By making your tendencies and patterns more conscious, you can actively choose how you behave. In reality, you are constantly deciding how to respond to your children, even if certain behaviors feel instinctual or personality-based.

Workbook Questions:

- Which positive parenting communication behaviors from the previous list come naturally to me?

- How do my children respond to the positive communication behaviors I use?

- Which negative parenting communication behaviors, including those from the list in this chapter, are creating conflict in my home?

- Which specific negative parenting behaviors would I like to change?

In addition to cultivating constructive behaviors and avoiding destructive ones, there are three other practices to support positive family communication and conflict management in your home: first, holding regular family meetings; second, establishing and upholding family rules; and third, practicing the four steps of clear, compassionate communication (also known as nonviolent communication).

Holding Regular Family Meetings

As my husband and I have discussed ways to strengthen our family and establish constructive patterns of communication and conflict resolution, we have turned to the Taylor tradition of holding regular family meetings. During the past several years, we've benefited from this family legacy that supports family organization, collaboration, ongoing discussion, and, most importantly, the strengthening of family relationships.

While I love and appreciate the family I grew up in, we rarely held family meetings. Fortunately, I married a man who participated in weekly family meetings with his large family, so he has mastered the family meeting habit that I have learned to develop over time.

My husband's family members, from the oldest to the very youngest, gathered to discuss schedules, chores, family issues, and any other topic affecting the family. My in-laws even kept a log of their discussions and decisions recorded by a child scribe in an official notebook.

Our family is a bit more laid-back in style. My husband, five kids, and I don't take extensive notes during our almost-weekly meetings, but we do gather in our living room regularly and make sure that each family member participates as much as possible. We follow a simple agenda that begins by recognizing family members for good behavior and kind deeds done for others. After that, we discuss upcoming events, topics of concern, updating of allowances, and whatever else Tom and I have discussed beforehand that requires family attention. These are imperfect and dynamic discussions: They often involve boys rolling around on the carpet, reprimands for said boys, and assigned seats next to a parent while we try to finish what's most important, such as topics like the calendar, upcoming activities, and behavioral concerns.

This extra step of planning agenda topics ahead of time helps to build family unity and is an important example of parent collaboration. As a couple, Tom and I have benefited from having organized time with each other to prepare so we have a clear focus and strategy for activities, discipline, and family priorities, rather than merely responding in a reactive way to whatever comes up. We hope that, over time, the kids will expect family meetings and be able to sit still longer if a topic demands further discussion.

Beyond our own family's experience, in recent years, many family advocates have encouraged parents to hold regular family meetings. I've made a list of guidelines based on the best practices recommended by many leading psychologists. These may help you establish the habit of family meetings that successfully involve all family members:

- Set a specific time and place to ensure consistency.

- Avoid lengthy meetings, especially with young children.

- Decide on a specific facilitator (usually a parent) to guide the family discussion.

- Make sure to focus on interests, ideas, and options, rather than people and emotions.

- Allow everyone, even the youngest children, to participate freely in the discussions.
- Be flexible in how you approach topics and the actual meetings themselves.

Workbook Questions:

- Have I ever held a family meeting? If so, how did it go and what did we talk about?
- Generally, what do I think about the idea of holding family meetings?
- What are the biggest challenges to holding family meetings in my home?

One of the first topics you might begin discussing in your family meetings is establishing and upholding family rules.

Establishing and Upholding Family Rules

Imagine that you're in your car and running late for a meeting. As you approach the main intersection before the expressway, you notice a long line of cars ahead of you. You say to yourself, "Dang it, the traffic lights are not working!" You slow down and try to figure out who's going first. You ask yourself, "What's the pattern we're following to cross the intersection?" Slowly, you move forward as people take turns. But, without the usual green arrow, when you reach the front of the left turn lane, no one gives you a chance to turn and enter the expressway.

You're frustrated at having to wait at the broken light. *How can I signal the other drivers that it is now my turn?* Finally, you dart into the intersection and make it across without getting hit by another driver who was busy texting on her cell phone. One small broken light and more than five minutes of waiting—to get through an intersection that normally takes two minutes at most—means that you are definitely going to be late. You feel annoyed, but assume traffic will flow smoothly from here.

"You are kidding me!" you say as you approach another broken traffic light with its long line of cars waiting to get through. Now, you need to call your coworker to tell her that you will be late to the meeting. A simple commute has turned into a real drag, requiring a lot more time and attention than you had expected, or had patience for.

Now, imagine you are the driver and all traffic lights have been removed from every intersection in your town. There are no roundabouts, police officers, or stop signs to guide your behavior, so you must negotiate interactions with every driver you encounter in an intersection. Not only will you face potential danger entering each intersection, but you will also experience delays in reaching your destination.

Homes without standard rules and expectations for behavior are like intersections without traffic lights, stop signs, or roundabouts. Without standard rules for behavior, we spend time at each "difference that matters" to satisfy people with conflicting goals, roles, and values. Developing standard codes of behavior for people living together in a household makes sense to streamline the everyday conflicts we all experience in communal living. In short, family rules are like traffic lights to guide day-to-day interactions with family members.

In our homes, we often try to operate without stated rules to guide our everyday interactions with each other. We regularly cross multiple social intersections of difference or conflict with each other. Despite these constant intersections of difference, we are often spending excess amounts of time trying to negotiate conflicts that could be addressed by general rules and guidelines for both parents' and children's behavior.

To begin managing sibling conflict, we might first look at the "legislation" within our homes. What are the laws or rules on the books, how were they created, and do they represent the interest of the people who are governed?

Workbook Questions

- What are the stated rules in my home?
- What are the unspoken rules in my home?
- How do I handle violation of property, privilege, and rules of respect?
- Who developed these rules, and how are they enforced?
- Which rules apply the same for every person living in the home?
- Which rules need to be legislated and adopted by all family members?

Most parents either assume everybody knows the rules and should follow them because of parental authority, or they create rules as they go in an ad hoc fashion. Perhaps, they don't consistently enforce the stated or unspoken rules, so they find themselves regularly fighting about home basics, including property rights, fairness, teasing, physical aggression, and respect. In short, many parents spin their wheels trying to deal with conflicts that could be better addressed through more democratic decision-making and consistently upholding the rules rather than through continual executive orders from parents.

Not every intersection needs a traffic light (or the penalty of a ticket for running through it). Perhaps a roundabout, a stop sign, or even a yield sign will provide the necessary guidance for how to proceed. Like using these traffic signals, we can learn how to interact in time-effective and safe ways that allow every traveler to reach their destination in safety. Family rules won't prevent the occasional need to negotiate with others about how to proceed over uncommon ground, but parents don't need to reinvent the wheel at every intersection or difference family members encounter in daily life. We also benefit from drafting the rules when emotions are calm rather than escalated.

Given the variety of conflicts we experience with each other in home life, we need to determine which types of conflicts or intersections of difference between people need to be "legislated" upfront. In addition, we need to consider which types of conflict require the more time-consuming, collaborative process of mediation.

As you mull over these questions, reflect on the idea that there are different branches within a democratic government: executive, judicial, and legislative. You will probably sense the need for all three functions to achieve effective family governance, and not just the executive and judicial functions performed by the parent. In short, we need to include children in the successful running of our families.

Returning to the idea of traffic signals to guide everyday driving situations at intersections, as a family, we might consider holding family meetings to discuss and create rules regarding the following areas of family life:

- Property rights
- Privileges
- Fairness
- Bedtimes
- Food
- Screaming, yelling, and crying
- Screen time (TV, computer, phone, music)
- Chores and other home responsibilities
- Homework
- Physical aggression
- Allowance
- Family communication (i.e., how we talk to each other)

No matter what rules you adopt as a family, you will continue to encounter new areas of conflict that require conflict resolution processes that family members know how to use and understand. Even when you develop and uphold well-developed family rules that guide everyday behavior, you may need to make changes to the rules or family practices. You can prepare for the conflicts that arise by learning and practicing conflict resolution approaches, like parent-led mediation.

Addressing dynamic conflict situations and creating contingency plans for times when the given rules fail will help everyone. You can use the following suggestions to guide you through when dealing with the changing nature of family life:

- Revise House Rules as Needed

- Hold regular family meetings to discuss ongoing individual and family needs.

- Consult and receive feedback from all family members about possible changes.

- Establish Processes for Resolving Conflicts Not Addressed by Family Rules

- Train All Family Members in Chosen Conflict Resolution Process

- Before implementing a process like mediation, train all members in techniques and skills.

- Provide for ongoing development of social skills in individual and family settings.

- Regularly Review Conflict Resolution Process for Effectiveness and Fairness
- Discuss conflict patterns and concerns in regular family meetings.
- Adapt conflict resolution processes to ongoing and changing family needs.

Practicing Clear and Compassionate Communication

Families benefit from having deliberate standards and values for family communication. Essentially, each family member needs to develop the ability to address individual needs appropriately and to constructively respond to other family members' feelings, interests, and goals to decrease conflict in the home. In the following example, Kim, a mother of six-year-old Jacob, practices nonviolent communication principles that helps meet her personal need to eat food off a clean kitchen table without shaming or distancing her son, Jacob, from her.

Jacob regularly leaves his shoes on the kitchen table. Kim can't stand this—it's infuriating to find his shoes on the table where the entire family eats their meals. No matter how many times she asks Jacob not to put his shoes on the table, he still does it. It seems as if he couldn't care less about something that clearly matters to her.

Jacob's mom doesn't want to ask Jacob nicely any more, but she learns a new method of making requests using the principles of nonviolent communication. Instead of the demanding that Jacob remove his shoes once again from the table, she starts with an observation about his behavior without the usual evaluation attached: "I've noticed that you leave your shoes on the kitchen table about once a day."

She then shares her feelings and acknowledges her personal needs. "I feel really upset when I see your shoes on the table because I know that those same shoes might have walked through mud, dog poop, and lots of other things before they wind up on our kitchen table. I need to eat on a clean kitchen table."

Finally, she makes a request—not a demand—that relates to what she has openly shared with Jacob. "So that I can feel comfortable eating food off our kitchen table, would you please not put your shoes on the table?"

Following weeks of nagging Jacob about his shoes, he suddenly shows understanding and quickly removes his shoes from the kitchen table. Months later, Jacob's mom has not seen his shoes on the table since that short discussion about her observation, feelings, expressed need, and clear-cut request. This is the power of nonviolent communication, which I call clear, compassionate communication.

The late psychologist, Dr. Marshall Rosenberg, claimed that it's not our needs that are in conflict, but the way we pursue our needs that creates conflict. To help people meet personal and other-focused needs, Rosenberg developed the principles of nonviolent communication that involves four, clear communication steps that support positive interaction and help form the foundation of successful parent-led mediation. (I've changed Dr. Rosenberg's term to "clear and compassionate communication" to emphasize the central goal of clear communication with family members.)

Rosenberg's communication techniques can diffuse conflict in the home because how family members speak to each other prevents, escalates, or de-escalates conflict. To develop relationships with family members based on honesty and empathy, we can apply the four following steps to communicate our sincere personal needs and make requests without putting the other person on the defensive.

1. **Make Observations, Not Evaluations**

   First, you state what you are seeing, hearing, or touching that is affecting your sense of well-being—without mixing in any evaluation. To be concrete and accurate, avoid generalizations, but instead ground your observations in time and context. For example, instead of "you never brush your teeth," you can say, "I noticed that two times this week you left for school without brushing your teeth." As we accurately account for what we have observed, we encourage others to share their observations without judgment.

2. **Express Your True Feelings**

   To clearly express your feelings, Rosenberg suggests developing a rich vocabulary of feelings (http://www.nonviolentcommunication.com/pdf_files/feelings_needs.pdf) that allow you to name or identify your emotions clearly and specifically. Expressing your feelings demonstrates your willingness to be vulnerable, a necessary step for collaboratively resolving conflicts.

While we are encouraged to use "I" statements that reflect what we are experiencing as individuals, be sure that these statements accurately reflect your own feelings and not just what you think someone feels about you. For example, when someone says, "I feel like you don't understand me," they're really making a judgment about the other person's ability to understand them. Rather than focus on the other person's perception of them, they need to focus on accurately expressing their own feelings and experiences. Instead, you could say, "I feel like I'm unclear in expressing how I'm doing right now."

3. **State Your Real Needs**

In clear, compassionate communication, we accept responsibility for our own feelings, recognizing that what others say and do may be the stimulus, but never the cause, of the feelings we have. In learning to state your true needs, you accept full responsibility for your intentions and actions, but not for the feelings of others.

In the example of the mother, Kim, with her son, Jacob, she stated her need to eat off a clean kitchen table. This may not be Jacob's need (maybe he doesn't mind eating off a dirty kitchen table), but Kim owned her need after stating her observation about Jacob's shoes on the table and expressing a feeling about her observation.

4. **Make Requests without Demanding Compliance**

   After making an observation, expressing your true feelings, and stating your needs, you are ready to make a request to the other party for actions that might fulfill your needs. Here you want to use concrete, specific, and positive language and avoid making demands or threats (requests are received as demands when listeners believe they will be blamed or punished if they don't comply).

   Rather than using a general request (and evaluation)—for example, "Jacob, could you not be so messy all the time?"—Kim asked a very specific question to try to meet her need for a clean kitchen table. She asked, "So that I can feel comfortable eating food off our kitchen table, would you please not put your shoes on table?" Jacob had the freedom to say yes or no, but he knew what she really wanted or needed from him. He was not judged for being a messy person, but rather, he was treated with respect by being asked a specific question that he could respond to appropriately.

In my personal life, I eliminated a lot of frustration in my life and met more personal needs by using the methods of clear and compassionate communication that Marshall advocates. By stating specific observations without judgments, followed by expressions of my real emotions and needs, I can make clear, concrete requests of others that reflect my true desires. With understanding that we rarely get what we want if we don't request it, this communication style has helped me address longstanding issues and has produced greater collaboration and positive results.

In addition, I've strengthened my relationships with friends and family because I have broached difficult subjects without the use of threats, demands, or even simple avoidance. We increase intimacy with loved ones as we constructively address our innermost needs and desires in positive ways. Each family member benefits from gaining greater skill while addressing true needs and responding to others who make requests using this communication style. These communication skills improve our ability to resolve conflict and support the central communication roles and processes of parent-led mediation, both for children and for parents.

As you supplement the principles of parent-led mediation with personal communications skill building, family meetings, family rules, and clear, compassionate communication, our family members can interact more peacefully and effectively with each other. All these practices take time and energy to implement, but by small and simple changes, we will experience great things over time in our families.

Chapter 10 Summary

1. **Building Parent Communications Skills**

Focus on developing the following positive parenting communication behaviors:

- Help your children not to blame each other (and avoid blaming one or both children yourself).
- Help your children see how his or her sibling feels about the conflict generally.
- Help your children to think of solutions to their conflicts.
- Help your children say what each child in the conflict wanted.
- Help your children make their own decisions about how the conflict should end.
- Help your children make sure that both children are happy with the chosen solution.

Refrain from the following negative parenting communication behaviors:

- Deciding how your children's conflicts should end
- Yelling at your children for fighting

- Ignoring your children while they are fighting
- Punishing your children for fighting
- Getting angry with your children when they fight
- Taking sides when your children are fighting
- Telling your children to work out the fight themselves (Siddiqui and Ross 2004)

2. **Holding Regular Family Meetings**
   - Set a specific time and place to ensure consistency.
   - Avoid lengthy meetings, especially with young children.
   - Decide on a specific facilitator (usually a parent) to guide the family discussion.
   - Focus on interests, ideas, and options, rather than people and emotions.
   - Allow everyone, even the youngest children, to participate freely in the discussions.
   - Be flexible in how you approach topics and the actual meetings themselves.

3. **Establish and Uphold Family Rules**

Revise House Rules as Needed
   - Hold regular family meetings to discuss ongoing individual and family needs.
   - Consult and receive feedback from all family

members about possible changes to the rules.

Establish Processes for Resolving Conflicts Not Addressed by Family Rules

Train All Family Members in Chosen Conflict Resolution Process

- Before implementing a process like mediation, train all family members in techniques and skills.
- Provide for ongoing social skills development in individual and family settings.

Review Conflict Resolution Process for Effectiveness and Fairness

- Discuss conflict patterns and concerns in regular family meetings.
- Adapt conflict resolution processes to ongoing and changing family needs.

4. **Practicing Clear, Compassionate Communication**
   - Make Observations, Not Evaluations
   - Express Your True Feelings
   - State Your Real Needs
   - Make Requests without Demanding Compliance

CHAPTER 11

CONCLUSION

We joke that life doesn't come with an instruction manual, but instead, we have mothers. I would include all parents: mothers, fathers, grandparents, and other caregivers. Through our parents, we learn the basic framework for social interactions, problem-solving, and dealing with the differences we encounter in our daily lives. As parents, we have the critical responsibility of teaching our children how to interact peaceably with each other and find happiness through growing, learning, and developing strong interpersonal relationships based on love and trust.

Given my worldview, I shifted my focus from studying international political problems to exploring how I can help raise a generation of children to become peacemakers in their own lives. This effort has helped me realize that no matter what I try to teach or tell my children, the living example I set will carry the most weight with them.

To raise a mediator, I must become a mediator, not just by what I say, but by how I behave as a parent. I demonstrate my commitment to teaching effective problem-solving, empathy, and perspective taking, not by my words, but by how I interact with my children and others each day. My values become explicit when my children observe how I react to their conflicts and my own. To be an effective teacher and guide to my children, I first seek to learn about managing conflict myself. Then, with a conscious awareness of my own patterns and a commitment to improve, I am ready to directly teach and model what I have learned with my children.

In 2015, as I put the finishing touches on a presentation for my final master's degree course, I surfed Google for quotes about the power of mediation, particularly for children. To my delight, in an instant, Google provided me with a fantastic quote by the Dalai Lama. I thought to myself, "Even one of the most well-known spiritual leaders on the planet recognizes the power of children learning mediation." Although I didn't use the quote in my presentation, I saved the image for future use.

If every child in the world would be
taught meditation,
We would eliminate violence from the world
within one generation.
The Dalai Lama

While preparing to write *Raising Mediators*, I pulled the quote up from my files and realized my rather large mistake in reading the quote accurately. The Dalai Lama quote refers to *meditation,* not *mediation.* Finally, I caught the spelling nuance, but I had already developed a strong view about the power of children learning mediation to reduce all types of violence in the world.

Like me, even search engines make the mistake—that of confusing meditation with mediation because the words look so similar. Most importantly, and a point that could easily be missed, search engines provide information about meditation because the literature on children and mediation is so limited among general options.

Indeed, without paying high fees for academic journal subscriptions, most of what's available on resolving sibling conflict would remain largely unknown. Consequently, despite my imperfection in implementing everything I have learned about resolving sibling conflict from my studies and daily life with five children, I have answered the call to write. I hope that by sharing the effectiveness of parent-led mediation in resolving sibling conflicts, your home life will improve and your children will be equipped to handle the conflicts and challenges they face in their lives constructively.

As I have mentioned throughout *Raising Mediators,* as opposed to the more solitary practice of meditation, parent-led mediation involves a collaborative communication process. As parent-mediators, we avoid judgment or evaluation of our children when they fight with each other. Instead, we assist our children with the TEACH ME steps of parent-led mediation:

- Time to Assess

- **E**stablish Structure
- **A**cknowledge Alternate Views
- **C**larify Emotions and Interests
- **H**ear All Ideas and Reframe Conflict
- **M**ake Joint Decisions
- **E**xpect Changes

This simple and structured communication process allows us to teach our children conflict management skills rather than leaving them to chance, peer influence, or hard life experience. As we assume the role of mediators with our children, we take responsibility for sharing critical communication skills, instead of assuming our children will somehow acquire a constructive and positive way to resolve the conflicts they encounter.

It seems appropriate to extend the Dalai Lama's message from the inner-focused practice of meditation to the social communication process of mediation. Parent-led mediation with our children provides a specific, interactive social process that helps eliminate violence in all its forms from our world, and particularly from our homes. With practice, we hope for not only more peaceful children, but more peaceful adults as we practice what we preach and watch our children mature into peace-making adults themselves.

APPENDIX

Recommendations for Understanding General Conflict Resolution Principles

*

Chapter-Based Resources and References

*

References for Further Study of Mediation, the Sibling Relationship, & Resolving Sibling Conflict

RESOURCES FOR FURTHER READING AND STUDY

RECOMMENDATIONS FOR UNDERSTANDING GENERAL CONFLICT RESOLUTION PRINCIPLES

Coleman, Peter T., and Morton Deutsch, eds. *The Handbook of Conflict Resolution: Theory and Practice.* 2014.

This updated anthology on conflict studies provides a sweeping overview of conflict studies topics from academics while suggesting practical applications for implementation.

Fisher, Roger and William Ury. *Getting to Yes: Negotiating Agreement without Giving In.* 2011.

This business negotiation classic lays out the fundamentals to facilitative negotiation that underscores all facilitative mediation processes.

Michael L. Spangle and Myra Warren Isenhart. *Negotiation: Communication for Diverse Settings.* 2003.

This very approachable guide to negotiation influenced the

layout of chapter 2, which focuses on the five general conflict approaches of avoiding, accommodating, compromising, competing, and collaborating.

CHAPTER-BASED RESOURCES AND REFERENCES

Introduction

Moving Beyond Shame

Best-selling author and social work professor Brené Brown has published significant research documenting the role of shame and vulnerability in our lives. Her most popular book titles include the following:

Daring Greatly: How the Courage to Be Vulnerable Transforms the Way We Live, Love, Parent, and Lead. 2015.

Rising Strong: How the Ability to Reset Transforms the Way We Live, Love, Parent, and Lead. 2017.

I Thought It Was Just Me (but It Isn't): Making the Journey from "What Will People Think?" to "I Am Enough." 2007.

Influence of the Sibling Relationship

See the chapter 5 resources for specific research studies on the influence of the sibling relationship.

Child Development Overview

See chapter 4 resources for more information on key child development markers for conflict management.

Parenting Tendencies with Managing Sibling Conflict

See chapter 6 resources for studies of parenting responses to sibling conflict.

Chapter 1: An Overview of Conflict

Conflict Fluency

LeBaron, Michelle. *Bridging Cultural Conflicts: A New Approach for a Changing World*. San Francisco: Jossey-Bass. 2003.

Dr. Michelle LeBaron is a tenured professor at the University of British Columbia (UBC) law faculty and director of the UBC Program on Dispute Resolution. LeBaron's book on bridging intercultural conflict influenced my thoughts about being skilled in each conflict situation, like a linguist traveling through foreign lands.

Understanding Conflict Origins

Bartos, Otomar J., and Paul Wehr. *Using Conflict Theory*. Cambridge: Cambridge University Press. 2002.

The late Dr. Otomar J. Bartos and Dr. Paul Wehr, both former professors at the University of Colorado at Boulder, explore the three main sources of incompatible goals that fuel most conflict. These three sources include contested resources, incompatible roles, and incompatible values.

Deutsch, Morton, Peter T. Coleman, and Eric C. Marcus. *The Handbook of Conflict Resolution: Theory and Practice*. San Francisco: Jossey-Bass. 2014.

In *The Handbook of Conflict Resolution: Theory and Practice*, conflict theorists Morton Deutsch, Peter Coleman, and Eric Marcus provide a series of articles with an overview of conflict studies topics from academics while suggesting practical applications.

Michael L. Spangle and Myra Warren Isenhart. *Negotiation: Communication for Diverse Settings*. Thousand Oaks: Sage Publications, Inc. 2003.

In *Negotiation: Communication for Diverse Settings*, Dr. Michael Spangle and Dr. Myra Isenhart, emeritus professors and conflict resolution practitioners, explore the topic of negotiation from different angles allowing the reader to understand negotiation broadly, but also within specific contexts.

Michael L. Spangle and Myra Warren Isenhart. *Collaborative Approaches to Resolving Conflict*. Thousand Oaks: Sage Publications, Inc. 2000.

In *Collaborative Approaches to Resolving Conflict*, Spangle and Isenhart identify sources of conflict beyond Bartos's and Wehr's three sources of goal incompatibility. They also explain that conflict may arise about what information counts, what procedures should be used for resolution, the degree of trust between parties, and particular communication styles.

Differentiating Between Constructive and Destructive Conflict Patterns

Deutsch, Morton. "Cooperation and Competition." In
  The Handbook of Conflict Resolution edited by
  Morton Deutsch and Peter T. Coleman, 21–40, San
  Francisco: Jossey-Bass. 2000.

In the 2000 edition of *The Handbook of Conflict Resolution*,
Morton Deutsch presents an interesting first chapter entitled,
"Cooperation and Competition," comparing competitive
and cooperative conflict management approaches. On pages
25–26, Deutsch lists the general outcomes for both competitive and cooperative approaches, which reflect the closing
statements of chapter 2 in *Raising Mediators*.

Michael L. Spangle and Myra Warren Isenhart. *Collaborative Approaches to Resolving Conflict.* Thousand Oaks:
  Sage Publications, Inc. 2000.

In *Collaborative Approaches to Resolving Conflict*, Spangle and
Isenhart discuss destructive and constructive conflict management patterns that produce very different results for both
groups and individuals.

Chapter 2: Five General Approaches to Conflict Management

Addressing People, Process, and Problem in Conflict

Beer, Jennifer E. and Eileen Stief. *The Mediator's Handbook.* Montpellier: New Society Publishers. 1998.

Dr. Jennifer E. Beer and Eileen Stief outline the practical steps of mediating a conflict in *The Mediator's Handbook*. Beer and Stief point out that all conflict management approaches address people, process, and problems in different ways.

Categorizing Conflict Management into Five General Approaches

Thomas, Kenneth W. and Ralph H. Kilmann. "Overview of the Thomas-Kilmann Conflict Mode Instrument (TKI)." Kilmanndiagnostics.com. http://www. kilmanndiagnostics.com/overview-thomas-kilmann-conflict-mode-instrument-tki (Accessed February 7, 2016).

While conflict theorists categorize conflict approaches in various ways, conflict theorists Dr. Kenneth W. Thomas and Dr. Ralph H. Kilmann emphasize that we have five general options for responding to conflict, which include avoiding, accommodating, compromising, competing, and collaborating. Thomas and Kilmann have developed a conflict approach assessment tool that may be purchased by individuals at their web site.

Spangle, Michael L. and Myra Warren Isenhart. *Collaborative Approaches to Resolving Conflict.* Thousand Oaks: Sage Publications, Inc. 2000.

In *Collaborative Approaches to Resolving Conflict*, Spangle and Isenhart provide clear, succinct definitions of each of the five general conflict management approaches. Specifically, in chapter 2 of *Collaborative Approaches to Resolving Conflict,* the authors provide a detailed overview of the approaches with a comparison of the conflict styles. They also explore pros, cons, and ideal conditions for each conflict management style

Three Main Types of Miscommunications

Perrin, Nick. "Effective Communication: 3 Types of Miscommunication." Performancecritical.com. http://performancecritical.com/effective-communication-3-types-miscommunication. (Accessed September 17, 2016).

In a brief article entitled "Effective Communication: 3 Types of Miscommunication," communications specialist Nick Perrin describes three main types of miscommunication: Misunderstanding, non-understanding, and misinterpretation.

Developing Conflict Fluency

LeBaron, Michelle. *Bridging Cultural Conflicts: A New Approach for a Changing World.* San Francisco: Jossey-Bass. 2003.

In her book focused on addressing cultural conflicts, Michelle LcBaron presents the idea of conflict fluency, which focuses on the ability to skillfully use various conflict approaches in appropriate contexts to achieve social goals.

Chapter 4: Overview of Child Development Milestones

The Fundamental Attribution Error

Aronson, Elliot. *The Social Animal.* New York. 1995.

In the classic social psychology text, *The Social Animal* (1995) Dr. Elliot Aronson, an eminent American social psychologist, discusses the fundamental attribution error. This concept explains our tendency to attribute others' faults to their character or personality while underestimating the influence of situation or environment on other people's behavior. This means that when we see someone doing something, we tend to think it relates to their *personality* rather than the *situation* the person might be in. Conversely, when we explain our own less-than-perfect behavior, we tend to emphasize the influence of situation rather attribute negative ideas to our personality or disposition.

Identifying Constructive Communication Skills

Communication Skills. "List of Communication Skills." Communicationskills.co.in. www.communicationskills.co.in/list-of-communication-skills.htm. (Accessed March 22, 2016).

There are many ways to decide which specific constructive communication skills to develop. I happened upon this outstanding resource on a website simply named "Communication Skills." The specific list of skills referred to in *Raising Mediators* can be found at the abovementioned web site.

Child Development Basics Influencing Children's Conflict Management Abilities

Sandy, Sandra V. "The Development of Conflict Resolution Skills: Preschool to Adulthood." In *The Handbook of Conflict Resolution: Theory and Practice*, edited by Coleman, Peter T., Morton Deutsch, and Eric C. Marcus, 430–463. San Francisco: John Wiley and Sons, Inc. 2014.

A researcher dedicated to studying children's developmental abilities, Dr. Sandra V. Sandy, explores child development basics for preschool through adolescent children so parents know what to expect from their children in managing conflict.

Holden, G.W. *Parenting: A Dynamic Perspective*. Los Angeles: Sage Publications. 2014.

In *Parenting: A Dynamic Perspective,* Professor Ethan W. Holden of Southern Methodist University provides an extensive overview of child development studies of preschoolers, school-aged children, and teenagers. Key chapters on child development specifics include 8–10.

Chapter 5: The Sibling Relationship and Sibling Conflict

Four Ways to Respond to Negative Messages

Rosenberg, Marshall. *Nonviolent Communication: A Language of Compassion.* PuddleDancer Press. 2003.

Dr. Marshall Rosenberg claimed there are four main ways people respond to the negative messages we receive and experience with others. He explores this topic in his book *Nonviolent Communication,* which is discussed further in the Chapter 10 resources.

The Sibling Relationship

In recent years, many child development and psychology studies have validated the importance of the sibling relationship. Key articles referenced in this chapter include the following:

Overview of Sibling Relationships

Howe, Nina, and Holly Recchia. "Siblings Relations and Their Impact on Children's Development." *Encyclo-*

pedia of Early Childhood Development (December 2014): 1. http://www.child-encyclopedia.com/sites/default/files/textes-experts/en/829/sibling-relations-and-their-impact-on-childrens-development.pdf. Accessed October 13, 2015.

In this article for the *Encyclopedia of Child Development*, Dr. Nina Howe and Dr. Holly Recchia of Concordia University provide an essential overview of research on sibling relations in relation to children's development.

Prosocial Development through Sibling Relationships

Kramer, Laurie. "The Essential Ingredients of Successful Sibling Relationships: An Emerging Framework for Advancing Theory and Practice." *Child Development Perspectives* 4, no. 2 (2010): 80-86.

Dr. Laurie F. Kramer, professor emerita from the Department of Human Development and Family Studies at the University of Illinois, investigated the potential for the sibling relationship to have a positive impact on an individual child's social and emotional development. In a study of eighty-eight, two-child and two-parent families, Kramer investigated the role of parent intervention in sibling conflict. Second-born children in the study were three to five years old with siblings ranging from two to four years older. Kramer's research suggests that ignoring sibling conflicts is associated with the occurrence of further conflict and that younger sibling pairs benefit the most from parent intervention in sibling conflict. Within her study, Kramer also includes a thought-provoking list of positive social behaviors that children can develop more fully through positive sibling relationships.

Sibling Relationship Quality Affecting Individual Child Development Outcomes

In two different studies, a research team led by Dr. Mark Feinberg, research professor of health and human development at Penn State University, and Dr. Anna Solmeyer, former researcher with the Family Relationships Project at Penn State University, investigated how the quality of sibling relationships influences how a child develops socially and emotionally.

Feinberg, Mark E., Anna R. Solmeyer, and Susan M.
 McHale. "The Third Rail of Family Systems: Sibling
 Relationships, Mental and Behavioral Health, and
 Preventive Intervention in Childhood and Adoles-
 cence." *Clinical Child and Family Psychology Review*
 15, no. 1 (March 2012): 43–57.

In this study, researchers investigated the current research on sibling relationships during childhood and adolescence. The team presents a model, which focuses on three key ways that siblings influence each other. The researchers suggest possible program ideas that can help children who are in dysfunctional or difficult sibling relationships.

Feinberg, Mark A., Anna R. Solmeyer, Michelle Hostetler,

Kari-Lyn Sakuma, Damon Jones, and Susan M. McHale. "Siblings are Special: Initial Test of a New Approach for Preventing Youth Behavior Problems." *Journal of Adolescent Health* 53 (2012): 166–173.

This research suggests that siblings and sibling relationships significantly influence children's development, mental health, and behavioral risk across childhood and adolescence. Based on this understanding, researchers developed and applied a randomized trial of Siblings Are Special (SIBS), a group-format afterschool program for fifth graders with a younger sibling in second through fourth grades. The children attended twelve weekly afterschool sessions and, along with their parents, three family nights. The program succeeded in enhancing positive sibling relationships, appropriate strategies for parenting siblings, child self-control, social competence, and academic performance. In addition, participation in the program was associated with reduced maternal depression and child internalizing problems.

Benefits of Conflict in Sibling Relationships

Ram, Avigail, and Hildy Ross. "'We Got to Figure It Out': Information sharing and Siblings' Negotiations of Conflicts of Interests." *Social Development* 17, no. 3 (2008): 512–527.

Kramer, L. "The Essential Ingredients of Successful Sibling Relationships: An Emerging Framework for

Advancing Theory and Practice." *Child Development Perspectives* no. 4 (2) (2010): 80–86.

Child development researchers confirm that, in moderate doses, sibling conflict provides key developmental opportunities for children.

Sibling Conflict

Martin, J., and H. Ross. "The Development of Aggression within Sibling Conflict." *Early Education & Development* 6 (1995): 335–358.

Perlman, Michal, and Hildy S. Ross. "The Benefits of Parent Intervention in Children's Disputes: An Examination of Concurrent Changes in Children's Fighting Styles." *Child Development* 68, no. 4 (August 1997): 690–700.

Perlman, M., and H.S. Ross. "If-Then Contingencies in Children's Sibling Conflicts." *Merrill-Palmer Quarterly* no. 51 (2005): 42–66.

Ross, H., J. Martin, M. Perlman, M. Smith, E. Blackmore, and J. Hunter. "Autonomy and Authority in the Resolution of Sibling Disputes." *New Directions for Child and Adolescent Development* no. 73 (Autumn) (1996): 71–90.

Ross, Hildy S., Rebecca E. Filyer, Susan P. Lollis, Michal Perlman, and Jacqueline L. Martin. "Administering

Justice in the Family." *Journal of Family Psychology* 8, no. 3 (1994): 254–273.

Siddiqui, Afshan A., and Hildy S. Ross. "How Do Sibling Conflicts End?" *Early Education & Development* 10 (3) (1999): 315–32.

Wilson, Anne E., Melissa D. Smith, Michael Ross, and Hildy S. Ross. "Young Children's Personal Accounts of Their Sibling Disputes." *Merrill-Palmer Quarterly*, no. 1 (2004):39–60.

Recchia, Holly E., and Nina Howe. "Sibling Relationship Quality Moderates the Associations between Parental Interventions and Siblings' Independent Conflict Strategies and Outcomes." *Journal of Family Psychology* 23, no. 4 (2009): 551–561. PsycINFO, EBSCOhost. Accessed September 25, 2015. http://0-dx.doi.org.bianca.penlib. du.edu/10.1037/a0014980.

Many researchers have begun investigating what issues siblings disagree about, how they tend to fight with each other, how frequently conflict arises, and how children resolve (or not) their conflicts with each other. Notably, professor emerita, Dr. Hildy Ross of the University of Waterloo, has made significant academic contributions to the study of children, sibling relationships, and conflict resolution.

Possible Sibling Conflict Endings

See chapter 8 resources for mediation studies results, especially Siddiqui and Ross (2004).

Conflict Resolution within Different Family Relationships

Recchia, Holly E., Hildy S. Ross, and Marcia Vickar.
"Power and Conflict Resolution in Sibling, Parent-Child, and Spousal Negotiations." *Journal of Family Psychology* 24, no. 5 (2010): 605–615.

Conflicts within different family relationships, such as parent-child, sibling, or spousal conflicts, tend to end differently based on which generations are interacting with each other. This study focused on examining conflict strategies (planning, opposition) and resolutions (standoff, win-loss, compromise) within different family relationships. Sixty-seven families with up to six different family subsystem pairings (children's ages ranged from three to twelve years) discussed an unresolved conflict. In general, the results revealed that within generation discussions (between siblings or spouses) ended more often in standoff, while conflicts between generations discussions (parent-child) ended with more win-loss resolutions. In general, family relationships that involved more planning and less opposition produced resolutions rather than failing to resolve differences.

Chapter 6: Patterns of Parent Response to Sibling Conflict

Dreikurs's Position to Ignore Sibling Conflict

Dreikurs, Rudolf. *Children: The Challenge.* New York: Hawthorne Books. 1964.

The best-selling parenting book in 1964 was one of Austrian psychiatrist and educator Rudolf Dreikurs' books entitled *Children: The Challenge.* Dreikurs asserted that sibling conflict is merely children's means of gaining parents' attention. More recent studies contradict Dreikurs's claim that parents should manage sibling conflict by ignoring it.

Investigating Parental Beliefs about and Response to Sibling Conflict

Most conflicts, whether in sibling, parent-child, or spousal relationships, do not ever get resolved. When conflicts are not resolved, they usually increase in frequency and even intensity. Many parents intend to help their children resolve conflict collaboratively, but often ignore their children's sibling conflicts and rely on this strategy three times more often than any others.

Kramer, Laurie, Lisa A., Perozynski, and Tsai-Yen Chung. "Parental Responses to Sibling Conflict: The Effects of Development and Parent Gender." *Child Development* 70, no. 6 (November/December 1999): 1401–1414.

Dr. Laurie F. Kramer, professor emerita of the University of Illinois, and the late Dr. Lisa A. Perozynski of the University of New Mexico at Carlsbad, carried out two studies that divided parenting strategies into three main groupings: control, child-centered, and passive nonintervention (ignoring). Researchers in this study used eighty-eight families (primarily Caucasian) with two parents and two children between the ages of three to five years in order to investigate the relationships between parent gender, conflict-strategy preference, and outcome on the sibling relationship. Key findings confirmed that parental intervention in sibling conflict decreases the likelihood of continued conflict, but intervention effectiveness depends on the strategy the parent chooses and the children's age and development. Younger sibling pairs benefited from parent intervention by either the mother or father.

Perozynski, Lisa, and Laurie Kramer. "Parental Beliefs about Managing Sibling Conflict." *Developmental Psychology* 35, no. 2 (1999): 489–499. PsycINFO, EBSCOhost. Accessed September 25, 2015. http://0-dx.doi.org.bianca.penlib.du.edu/10.1037/0012-1649.35.2.489.

In this related research study of eighty-eight primarily Caucasian, two-parent American families with two children between the ages of three to five, Perozynski and Kramer reported that parents' use of certain strategies to resolve sibling conflict was based in part on the parents' perception of how effective the strategy was and how well they could apply it. Despite parents' belief that child-centered and control strategies were more effective strategies for their children, parents used passive nonintervention or ignoring sibling three times as often as the other two methods. Also, mothers and fathers not only intervened differently, but also held different beliefs about how to manage their children's conflicts. Fathers tended to prefer control strategies, while mothers reported similar confidence in using either control or child-centered strategies.

Positive Impact of Parent Intervention in Siblings Conflicts

Research demonstrates the positive impact of parent intervention in many types of sibling conflict.

Perlman, Michal, and Hildy S. Ross. "The Benefits of Parent Intervention in Children's Disputes: An Examination of Concurrent Changes in Children's Fighting Styles." *Child Development* 68, no. 4 (August: 1997): 690–700.

Through a study of forty, two-parent, English-speaking Canadian families with at least two children between the ages of two and four, Michael Perlman and Hildy S. Ross investigated how parental intervention in sibling conflict among preschoolers affects conflict outcomes for children. Researchers collected data on conflict behavior through six, ninety-minute sessions in the homes of each of the study families, including more than 2,200 conflicts. Parents intervened in 57 percent of these conflicts, providing clear, immediate benefits to how constructively children worked through conflict with each other (e.g., less opposing of each other, fewer attempts to use power over another, less crying, with more children's reasoning, perspective taking, and compliance). Parent intervention among preschoolers appears to decrease conflict intensity and encourage more sophisticated conflict behaviors, especially among the older siblings involved in the study.

Dunn, Judy, and Penny Munn. "Sibling Quarrels and
Maternal Intervention: Individual Differences in
Understanding and Aggression." *Journal of Child
Psychology and Psychiatry* 27, no. 5 (September 1986):
583–595.

This 1986 study also confirmed the positive influence of parents intervening in their younger children's conflicts.

Herrera, C., and Judy Dunn. "Early Experiences with
Family Conflict: Implications for Arguments with
a Close Friend." *Developmental Psychology*, no. 33
(1997): 869-881.

Herrara and Dunn's research suggests that a mother's use of other-focused reasoning is more strongly correlated with her child's later conflict management style than with the child's early argument style as a youth.

Differing Parent Response Based upon Attributions of Guilt

In research settings, when parents assumed that one child was guilty of causing the conflict, they used control strategies for conflict management. However, when parents did not know which child to blame, they used more collaborative methods, including questions, restatements, and discussion.

Recchia, Holly E., Cecilia Wainryb, and Nina Howe.
"Two Sides to Every Story?: Parents' Attributions of Culpability and Their Interventions into Sibling Conflict." *Merrill-Palmer Quarterly* 59, no. 1 (January 2013): 1–22.

In this study featuring 61 sibling pairs (ranging from four to ten years old) and their primary caregivers (53 mothers, seven fathers, and one legal guardian), Recchia, Wainryb, and Howe investigated the links between parents assigning blame in recurring sibling conflict and choice of intervention strategy. When parents judged one child to be solely to blame for sibling conflict, parents intervened with little attention to the children's differing states of mind, or rarely engaged in helping children understand each other's perspectives. But, if parents assumed that both children were at fault, they intervened with more references to children's conflicting goals, perspectives, and environmental factors. Parents tended to help their younger children express their sides of the story, but were equally likely to support evidence in favor of either the older or younger sibling.

Warning about Preferential Treatment by Parents

Howe, Nina, and Holly Recchia. "Sibling Relationships as
a Context for Learning and Development." *Early
Education and Development* 25.2 (2014): 155–159.

Child development researchers Howe and Recchia chronicle
the negative effect that preferential treatment of one sibling
over another has on the overall quality of sibling relationships.

Chapter 7: Analyzing Parent Conflict Management Approaches in Context

As a mother and conflict resolution specialist, I developed
the TEACH ME acronym to help parents and children
remember certain information, but used the specific words
TEACH ME to emphasize that children and parents can
learn more constructive strategies for dealing with conflicts.
Parents can help their children by first learning the parent-
focused TEACH ME steps to managing conflict in chapter
7, then reuse the acronym in chapter 8 to learn parent-led
mediation steps.

Research about Parents Intervening or Choosing Not to Intervene in Sibling Conflict

Kramer, Laurie, Lisa A., Perozynski, and Tsai-Yen Chung.
"Parental Responses to Sibling Conflict: The Effects
of Development and Parent Gender." *Child Development* 70, no. 6 (November/December 1999):
1401–1414.

Perozynski, Lisa, and Laurie Kramer. "Parental Beliefs about Managing Sibling Conflict." *Developmental Psychology* 35, no. 2 (1999): 489–499. PsycINFO, EBSCOhost. Accessed September 25, 2015. http://0-dx.doi.org.bianca.penlib. du.edu/10.1037/0012-1649.35.2.489

Two studies by Kramer and Perozynski, which are summarized in the chapter 6 resources, reveal that parents often do not help their children through their conflicts, which usually results in more conflict in the future. Parents often ignore sibling conflict, even though they agree that child-centered approaches to conflict would be more appropriate or helpful.

Results of Choosing Not to Intervene in Sibling Conflict

Perlman, Michal, and Hildy S. Ross. "The Benefits of Parent Intervention in Children's Disputes: An Examination of Concurrent Changes in Children's Fighting Styles." *Child Development* 68, no. 4 (August 1997): 690–700.

Research confirms that when we leave our children to their own problem-solving devices following a conflict, both younger and older sibling pairs tend to experience increased conflict and hostility toward each other. See chapter 6 resources discussing the following article listed above this paragraph.

Parent Tendency toward Blaming One Child

Recchia, Holly E., Cecilia Wainryb, and Nina Howe.
"Two Sides to Every Story?: Parents' Attributions
of Culpability and Their Interventions into Sibling
Conflict." *Merrill-Palmer Quarterly* 59, no. 1
(January 2013): 1–22.

Please refer to the summary presented in the chapter 4
endnotes about research by Recchia, Wainryb, and Howe.
There you will find further details about parental tendencies
to blame one child over another.

Parents Perpetuating an Original Conflict Management Choice

Kramer, Laurie, Lisa A., Perozynski, and Tsai-Yen Chung.
"Parental Responses to Sibling Conflict: The Effects
of Development and Parent Gender." *Child Development* 70, no. 6 (November/December 1999):
1401–1414.

Research suggests that once parents have chosen and used
one conflict management strategy, they tend to use the same
strategy as the conflict continues or reoccurs in the future. In
short, the first conflict management choice tends to predict
our later choices for conflict management style. See the article
listed above for more details.

Parent-Led Mediation Benefits over Typical Parent Conflict Resolution Methods

See chapter 8 resources for more details about research by Siddiqui and Ross (2004), Smith and Ross (2007), and Ross and Lazinski (2014) focused on parent-led mediation benefits.

Chapter 8: Introduction to Parent-led Mediation
Parent & Child Ability to Learn and Preference for Mediation.

In several studies, parents and children voiced preference for mediation practices over typical patterns of parent involvement. Research demonstrates that both parents and children learn mediation skills readily.

Siddiqui, Afshan, and Hildy Ross. "Mediation as a Method of Parent Intervention in Children's Disputes." *Journal of Family Psychology* 18, no. 1 (March 2004): 147–159.

In this study of forty-eight English-speaking Canadian families (mothers with two children, averaging in age between five and eight years), Siddiqui and Ross demonstrated that mediation-trained mothers could successfully use mediation to resolve their children's conflicts and empower younger siblings to solve conflict issues. Not only did the mothers and children prefer mediation, but the study also suggests that mediation promotes children's socio-cognitive development.

Child Preference for Mediation with Increased Collaborative Outcomes, and Strengthened Perspective-Taking and Empathy Skills

Smith, Julie L. "Effects of Parent Mediation in Sibling
  Disputes on Children's Socio-cognitive Skills and
  Conflict Interactions." PhD diss., University of
  Waterloo. 2005. Accessed September 18, 2015.

Julie Smith's PhD dissertation from the University of Waterloo expanded research findings from Siddiqui and Ross's 2004 study of parent-led mediation. Smith's dissertation forms the basis for Smith and Ross's 2007 research study documenting the benefits of parent-led mediation in the home. Further investigation of Smith's dissertation research reveals nuances of the 2007 Smith and Ross report, including the following insights: resolutions developed by children with parent's help in mediation group were often more constructive than resolutions developed by parents alone in the control group. Parents tended to use mediation in more severe conflicts, and there were no substantial differences between family members' level of satisfaction between mediated and control group families conflict outcomes Even without parents present, children as young as three years old could resolve almost as many conflicts as their older siblings. Finally, children from the mediation group demonstrated a significantly higher ability to understand the perspective of the other person in the conflict.

Empowered Younger Siblings Benefit from Mediating with Older Siblings

Smith, Julie, and Hildy Ross. "Training Parents to Mediate Sibling Disputes Affects Children's Negotiation and Conflict Understanding." *Child Development* 78, no. 3 (May/June 2007): 790–805.

Smith and Ross' 2007 study highlights the expanding benefits of parent-led mediation that included training for both mothers and fathers, rather than just mothers. Younger siblings experienced greater participation, more influence on conflict outcomes, and, ultimately, more favorable outcomes in resolving conflicts using parent-led mediation. Smith and Ross (2007) expanded upon Siddiqui and Ross's 2004 empirical research in a study of forty-eight Canadian families with two parents living at home. Both parents (not just mothers) were trained to mediate the conflicts between their siblings ranging from ages five to ten years old. Parents in the control group were instructed to intervene as they normally would, but despite mediation training, mediation parents did not intervene with mediation tactics unless their children's experienced more severe conflicts. Children in both conditions resolved issues in a mutually beneficial way by compromising, but the control group resolutions tended to favor older siblings. In mediation families, younger siblings were empowered to play an active role, and both older and younger siblings could better identify their siblings' perspectives on the conflict. Parents reported continued improvement in children's conflict resolution after the study, but the study did not include substantial follow-up assessments to understand the long-term effects of parent conflict mediation.

Parent-Led Mediation Empowers Younger Siblings and Facilitates Child Collaboration Even without Parents' Presence

Ross, Hildy S., and Marysia J. Lazinski. "Parent Mediation
Empowers Sibling Conflict Resolution." *Early
Education and Development* 25, no. 2 (2014):
259–275. Accessed September 16, 2015. http://
dx.doi.org/10.1080/10409289.2013.788425

When parents used parent-led mediation with their preschoolers to ten-year-old children, siblings resolved their differences more collaboratively with greater balance between older and younger siblings than children in the control group. Seven months after the research study, children still demonstrated greater collaborative skills without their parents' assistance or presence than control group children. In this study, Ross and Lazinski confirmed the research findings of Smith and Ross (2007) and Siddiqui and Ross (2004) to demonstrate that parents trained in mediation can effectively reduce their children's sibling conflict and develop children's ability to see another person's perspective on a particular conflict. In this study of fifty-eight Canadian families (forty-eight with both parents residing in home, ten either divorced or separated) with at least two children between the ages of three-and-a-half to ten years old, both parents were trained in mediation and participated in three separate lab studies over a period of approximately seven months. In the mediation group, younger siblings' interests and emotions were given greater attention, while in control groups, older siblings tended to dominate and were more likely to "win" the disputes despite parent participation.

Chapter 9: Implementing Parent-led Mediation

Questions to Determine Whether to Mediate

Kilmann, Ralph H. "Using the Thomas-Kilmann Conflict Mode Instrument (TKI)." Kilmanndiagnostics. com. http://www.kilmanndiagnostics.com/over-view-thomas-kilmann-conflict-mode-instrument (Accessed February 7, 2016).

Conflict theorists Thomas and Kilmann developed a simple set of questions to help people know how to select an appropriate conflict management approach for a given situation. I modified their list from the original eight questions found at http://www.kilmanndiagnostics.com/using-thomas-kilmann-conflict-mode-instrument.

Modifying the Haddon Matrix for Conflict

Heath, Chip and Dan Heath. *Decisive: How to Make Better Choices in Life and Work.* New York: Crown Business. 2013.

I was first exposed to the Haddon Matrix in the business management book *Decisive* by Chip and Dan Heath. The Heath Brothers modified the Haddon Matrix developed by injury-prevention expert William Haddon to support their decision-making application. I also borrowed ideas from the Haddon Matrix to create the Conflict Matrix.

Benefit of Reviewing Past Conflicts with Children

Schermerhorn, Alice C., Chow, Sy-Miin, and Mark E. Cummings. "Developmental Family Processes and Interparental Conflict: Patterns of Micro-Level Influences." *Developmental Psychology* 46, no. 4 (July 2010): 869–885.

Research confirms that children benefit from reviewing past conflicts, even those that did not necessarily end well.

Beware of Exhibiting Preferential Treatment toward One Sibling over Another

McHale, Susan M., Ann C. Crouter, Shirley A. McGuire, and Kimberly A. Updegraff. "Congruence Between Mothers' and Fathers' Differential Treatment of Siblings: Links with Family Relations and Children's Well-Being." *Child Development* 66, no. 1 (1995): 116–128.

Parents tend to avoid overcompensating for a younger or less mature sibling's attributes to avoid being considered unfair or biased in any way. Preferential parent treatment of one child over another may damage sibling relationship and individual child well-being in significant ways.

Autonomous Child Mediation with Siblings

In research settings, children effectively mediated conflicts without their parents present nearly seven months after first learning mediation strategies directly from their parents. See Ross & Lazinski (2014) in the chapter 6 resources.

The Power of Peer Mediation Programs with Adolescents

Burrell, N. A., Zirbel, C. S., & Allen, M. Evaluating peer mediation outcomes in educational settings: A meta-analytic review. *Conflict Resolution Quarterly*, *21*(1) (2003). 7–26.

Adolescents can develop a variety of effective communication skills through participating in peer mediation training programs. Most research evaluating adolescents' use of mediation principles focuses on peer mediation (rather than parent-led). Researchers have reviewed many studies to conclude that not only does peer mediation lead to an agreement nearly 94 percent of the time, but is widely preferred by participants with an 89 percent satisfaction rate.

Adolescent Socio-Cognitive Development

Sandy, Sandra V. "The Development of Conflict Resolution Skills: Preschool to Adulthood." In *Handbook*

of Conflict Resolution: Theory and Practice, edited by
Coleman, Peter T., Morton Deutsch, and Eric C.
Marcus, 430–463. San Francisco: John Wiley and
Sons, Inc. 2014.

Sandy discusses adolescent children's socio-cognitive development and how it affects their ability to successfully manage conflicts in relation to their capacity for successful conflict management.

Chapter 10: Family Practices That Support Effective Parent-Led Mediation

Parent Communication Skill Building

The positive and negative parent behaviors found in these lists either support or weaken parent-led mediation and are based upon the results of studies by Siddiqui & Ross (2004), Smith & Ross (2007), and Ross & Lazinski (2014).

Holding Regular Family Meetings

Goldsmith, Barton. "Ten Tips for Holding a Family
Meeting." Psychologytoday.com. https://
www.psychologytoday.com/blog/emotional-
fitness/201209/10-tips-holding-family-meeting
(Accessed January 25, 2016).

Dr. Barton Goldsmith, a well-known psychotherapist from California, shared ten clear guidelines for holding family meetings in *Psychology Today*.

Practicing Nonviolent Communication (Clear, Compassionate Communication)

Rosenberg, Marshall B. *Nonviolent Communication*. Puddle-
Dancer Press. 2003.

Dr. Marshall Rosenberg developed a four-step process for
making requests based on observations, expression of feelings,
and needs followed by a nonthreatening request.

FOR FURTHER STUDY OF MEDIATION, THE SIBLING RELATIONSHIP, AND RESOLVING SIBLING CONFLICT

Clifford, Edward. "Discipline in the Home: A Controlled
Observational Study of Parental Practices." *The
Journal of Genetic Psychology* 95, no. 1 (1959):
45–82.

Ducharme, Jennifer Lynn. 2003. "Associations Between
Parental and Sibling Family Subsystems and Ado-
lescent Externalizing and Internalizing Problems."
Ph.D. diss., Concordia University.

Dunn, Judy, and Cheryl Slomkowski. "Conflict and the
Development of Social Understanding." In *Conflict
in Child and Adolescent Development*, 70–92. New
York, NY, US: Cambridge University Press. 1992.

Feinberg, Mark E., Anna R. Solmeyer, and Susan M.
McHale. "The Third Rail of Family Systems: Sibling

Relationships, Mental and Behavioral Health, and Preventive Intervention in Childhood and Adolescence." *Clinical Child and Family Psychology Review* 15, no. 1 (March 2012): 43–57.

Feinberg, Mark A., Anna R. Solmeyer, Michelle Hostetler, Kari-Lyn Sakuma, Damon Jones, and Susan M. McHale. "Siblings are Special: Initial Test of a New Approach for Preventing Youth Behavior Problems." *Journal of Adolescent Health* 53 (2012): 166–173.

Hall, Jill. "Survey Shows How Mediation Can Be Successful." Mediate.com, September 2012. Accessed September 19, 2015. http://www.mediate.com/pfriendly.cfm?id=9935.

Hernandez, Marc W. "Learning to Understand and Resolve Family Conflict: The Effects of Mediation Training on Mother-Child Conflict Resolution." Ph.D. diss., University of Chicago. 2009.

Kressel, Tomneth. "Mediation." In *Handbook of Conflict Resolution: Theory and Practice*, edited by Morton Deutsch and Peter T. Coleman, 522–545. San Francisco: Jossey-Bass, Inc. 2000.

McHale, Susan M., Kimberly A. Updegraff, Corrina J. Tucker and Ann C. Crouter. "Step in or Stay Out? Parents' Roles in Adolescent Siblings' Relationships." *Journal of Marriage and Family* 62 (August 2000): 746–760.

Moore, Adelia. "Sibling Conflict and Parental Intervention in Middle Childhood: A Study of Parents' Beliefs, Perceptions and Reported Behavior. Ph.D. diss., University of Cincinnati.

Moore, Christopher W. 2014. *The Mediation Process: Practical Strategies for Resolving Conflict.* 4th ed. US: Jossey Bass Ltd. 1995.

Perlman, Michal, and Hildy S. Ross. "Who's the Boss? Parents' Failed Attempts to Influence the Outcomes of Conflicts between Their Children." *Journal of Social and Personal Relationships* 14, no. 4 (1994): 463–480. *PsycINFO*, EBSCO*host* (accessed September 26, 2015).

Recchia, Holly E., and Nina Howe. "Sibling Relationship Quality Moderates the Associations between Parental Interventions and Siblings' Independent Conflict Strategies and Outcomes." *Journal of Family Psychology* 23, no. 4 (2009): 551–561. PsycINFO, EBSCOhost. Accessed September 25, 2015. http://0-dx.doi.org.bianca.penlib.du.edu/10.1037/a0014980.

Ross, H., J. Martin, M. Perlman, M. Smith, E. Blackmore, and J. Hunter. "Autonomy and Authority in the Resolution of Sibling Disputes. *New Directions for Child and Adolescent Development* 1996, no. 73 (Autumn 1996): 71–90.

Ross, Hildy, Caroline Tesla, Brenda Kenyon, and Susan Lollis. "Maternal Intervention in Toddler Peer Conflict: The Socialization of Principles of Justice." *Developmental Psychology* 26, no. 6L (1990): 994–1003.

Siddiqui, Afshan. "Mediation as a Method of Parent Intervention in Sibling Disputes." PhD diss., University of Waterloo. 2002.

Smith, Melinda. "Mediation for Children, Youth, and Families: A Service Continuum." *Mediation Quarterly* 12 (1995): 55–74.

Tucker, Corinna Jenkins, and Kerry Kazura. "Parental Responses to School-aged Children's Sibling Conflict." *Journal of Child and Family Studies* 22, no.5 (2013): 737–745.

Turner, Elizabeth Kristine. "Learning How to Fight: Connections between Conflict Resolution Patterns in Marital and Sibling relationships." Ph.D. diss., University of Massachusetts Amherst. 2008.

Made in the USA
Columbia, SC
27 October 2020